BEEF

LIGHT, LEAN BEEF RECIPES FOR CONTEMPORARY LIFESTYLES

By Karen Chase & Tracy Bell

Illustrated by Karen Chase

Dedicated To

The many thousands of men and women and their families who know the lonely vigil of calving and the overwhelming sense of joy and fulfillment when the last one is up and running.

BEEF
LIGHT, LEAN BEEF RECIPES FOR CONTEMPORARY LIFESTYLES
by
Karen Chase & Tracy Bell

First Printing — September, 1986

Canadian Cataloguing in Publication Data
Chase, Karen
Beef, light lean beef recipes for contemporary lifestyles

Includes index.
ISBN 0-919845-47-9

1. Cookery (Beef). I. Bell, Tracy   II. Title.
TX749.C42 1986   641.6'62   C86-098060-X

Flowers Courtesy Of
Oak Bay Florist — Nola Merchant
2515 - 90 Avenue S.W., Calgary

Dishes And Accessories Courtesy Of
Bowring Brothers Limited
Chinook Centre, Calgary

Birks Jewellers
Chinook Centre, Calgary

Wine Information Courtesy of
J. Webb — Wine Merchant Ltd.
Glenmore Landing, Calgary

Photography by
Ross C. (Hutch) Hutchinson
Bolli & Hutchinson Photographic Design Ltd.
Calgary, Alberta

Designed, Printed and Produced in Canada by
Centax of Canada
Publishing Consultant and Food Stylist: Margo Embury
Design by: Blair Fraser
1048 Fleury Street
Regina, Saskatchewan, Canada   S4N 4W8
(306) 359-3737 Toll Free 1-800-667-5844

#105 - 4711 13 Street N.E.
Calgary, Alberta, Canada   T2E 6M3

TABLE OF CONTENTS

THANKS

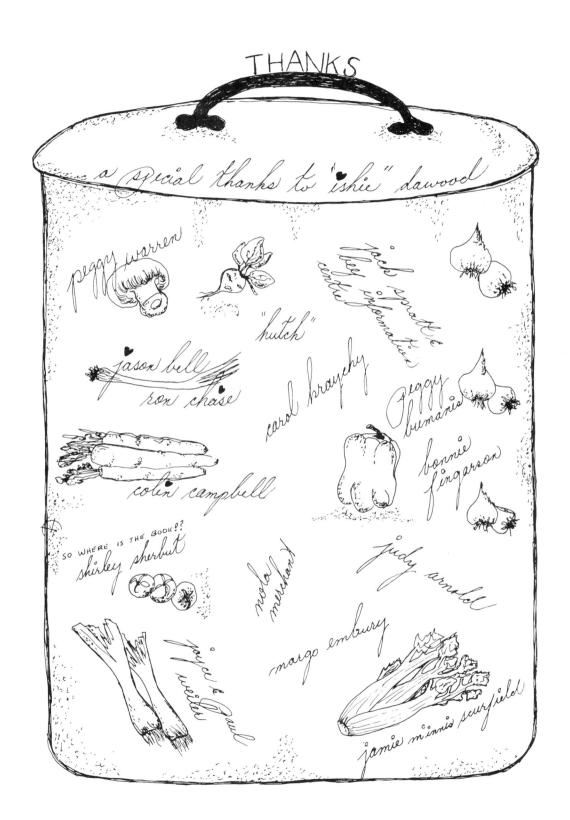

a special thanks to "ishie" dawood

peggy warren

jack sprattle they inform centre information

"hutch"

jason bell

ron chase

carol brayshy

peggy bumanis

bonnie fingarson

colin campbell

SO WHERE IS THE BOOK?!?

shirley sherbut

nola merchant

judy arnold

margo embury

joyce & paul weiler

jamie minnis scurfield

4

NEW NEWS . . . GOOD NEWS!
TODAY'S BEEF: NOW 35% LEANER

In 1972, the Canadian government changed the beef carcass grading system to greatly reduce the allowable amount of animal fat cover and intramuscular fat.

This means that Canadian producers have, over the past 14 years, through better feeding and breeding methods, produced a much leaner beef product which is completely compatible with the Canadian consumer's demand for . . . *lean and light, taste, healthfulness, nutrition, versatility and convenience. What a great boon for the health-oriented, physically active, consumer of today.

Canadian beef producers attempt to bring their animals to market in a condition that will achieve an 'A1' grade, which is not only the leanest and best grade but also the most profitable for the producer.

In 1985, 67% of beef animals marketed in Canada graded 'A'. Boneless beef used in processed meat and hamburgers represents another 25% of total marketings.

So enjoy, enjoy, enjoy . . . Canadian produced *lean beef! As a result of our unique grading system it is 'decidedly different' and, of course, 'better' than beef produced anywhere else in the world!

BEEF CUTS

New, Canadian-produced lean beef offers unsurpassed quality with well in excess of 25 different cuts to choose from at a variety of prices. There is a cut for every purpose, every occasion and for every budget. It's the unmatched versatility and incredible taste of beef that causes so many families to ask for beef again, and again, and again!

RIB — tender cuts
Removing the short-rib ends produces a tender seven-rib roast that may be divided into smaller roasts and steaks; those nearest the short loin being the most tender. Beef cuts from the rib area lend themselves equally to ROASTING, BROILING, GRILLING OR FRYING.

CHUCK — medium-tender cuts
Much of this fibrous section becomes blade steaks and roasts, as well as cross-rib roasts, all of which are BEST BRAISED. Stew beef, lean short ribs and ground beef account for the rest of this cut.

FORESHANK — less-tender cuts
Flavorful meat used for stews, or sliced into marrow-filled shank crosscuts for BRAISING or making bouillon stock.

BRISKET — less-tender cuts
The brisket 'first cut' has less fat and the pointed 'front cut' has more flavor . . . BEST BRAISED.

PLATE — less-tender cuts
The top part of this section is sold as short ribs. The rest is used for stew beef and ground beef . . . BEST BRAISED.

BEEF CUTS

When judging how tender or flavorful a cut of beef will be, it helps to know what part of the carcass it comes from. Meat from the front and rear sections are the tastiest while cuts from along the backbone are the most tender.

LOIN — tender-cuts
When this section is sliced crosswise, the bone-in steaks become more tender as they near the sirloin — improving from top loin, to T-bone to porterhouse. If divided lengthwise, the bottom part is the most tender of beef — tenderloin! Beef cuts from the loin can be enjoyed ROASTED, BROILED, GRILLED OR PAN FRIED.

SIRLOIN — tender-cuts
Deliciously tender steaks come from this region and can be BROILED, GRILLED and PAN FRIED.

ROUND — medium-tender cuts
This section provides a rump roast, inside (top), outside (bottom) round roasts or steaks. The heel and eye-of-the-round yield lean meat that is BEST BRAISED.

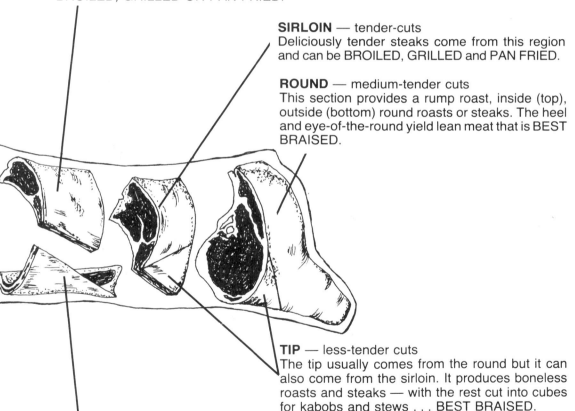

TIP — less-tender cuts
The tip usually comes from the round but it can also come from the sirloin. It produces boneless roasts and steaks — with the rest cut into cubes for kabobs and stews . . . BEST BRAISED.

FLANK — less-tender cut
The lean flank steak comes from the inner wall of this cut and is BEST BRAISED. The steak is frequently scored to tenderize it. The meat surrounding the steak is ground for hamburger.

PREPARING BEEF TO EXQUISITE PERFECTION

BEEF has, since ancient times, been at the center of celebration and feast.

Traditionally, hot coals or an open fire provided a dry heat that **ROASTED** beef to perfection. Today, we use an oven to furnish that dry heat. Tender beef cuts (see chart, page 6) such as tenderloin, are best suited to a roasting method that starts the process at a searing heat and continues at a moderate rate. Less tender cuts, such as chuck roasts, benefit from a low-heat roasting method that prevents drying out before the tenderizing action of the cooking has taken place. A roasting guide for beef is on pages 15 and 22.

BROILING AND BARBECUING are also dry-heat methods of cooking beef. They are, therefore, best suited to naturally tender beef cuts such as steaks. Please refer to page 11 for more information.

Beef cuts benefitting from the **BRAISING** method of using moisture to 'marry' flavors are less tender cuts from the shoulder and neck (see chart, page 6). Braising allows for the total immersion of beef in liquid, or if only a few spoonfuls of liquid are used in a snug Dutch oven, an aromatic concentration of flavors will occur. 'Pot roasting' is another expression used to describe the braising method.

The **FRYING** method of cooking beef is technically a 'dry' heat method. Therefore, only tender, quick-cooking cuts of beef are suitable. Pan frying is successful only when the size of the pan is equal to the job to be done. The pan should hold the meat snugly. If the pan is too big, fat and juices burn in areas not covered by meat. Crowding the beef traps juices in the bottom of the pan and the meat stews instead of searing.

Preparing beef in the **MICROWAVE** allows for a great deal of innovation and variation. Roasting times and hints are to be found on pages 15-17.

Beef at its natural best — **RAW** — requires only tenderizing. Carpaccio Steak, a 20th century rendition, differs from its predecessor, Steak Tartar, only in terms of tenderizing methods. We're told that 13th-Century Mongolian Tartars placed pieces of raw beef under their saddles at daybreak. After a day of hard riding the beef was thoroughly tenderized and perfect for instant eating. Carpaccio steak recipe can be found on page 50.

THE MAGIC OF MARINADE

Marinating both tenderizes and adds flavor to any beef cut.

Marinades work effectively through the use of an acid. Frequently used acids include fruit juices, vinegar, wine, beer, etc. It is the acid that helps to soften the connective tissues found in beef.

It is necessary to pierce holes in steaks and roasts or cut diagonal slashes in the meat to ensure that the marinade has an opportunity to penetrate and soften connective tissues throughout the entire beef cut.

Although marinades make magic, they do take time to work. The larger the cut of beef the longer you must marinate it. Less tender cuts such as short ribs must also be marinated longer.

Cubes and strips of beef need about 3-6 hours, while steaks and roasts should be marinated for 12-24 hours. All marinating should take place in the refrigerator.

*LEAN beef cuts that would be enhanced with a marinade include rump roast, round roast and round steak, sirloin tip roast and steak, eye of the round roast and flank steaks.

YOU CAN MAKE MAGIC

1. By choosing a small shallow bowl or tightly sealed plastic bag so marinade covers meat.

2. By turning the meat occasionally to expose all areas to the marinade.

3. By always covering and refrigerating.

4. By draining the meat on towelling before cooking to remove excess oil.

5. By remembering that time is the key . . . so marinate the required time.

6. Thawing the meat in a marinade is possible. While it does take longer to tenderize — there is less loss of meat juices.

MARINADE WIZARDRY

ACID to soften connective tissues: ½ cup (125 mL) acid such as cider vinegar, white vinegar, dry red wine, lemon juice, pineapple juice, tomato juice, beer, etc.

PLUS

OIL to act as an adherent between marinade and meat: ½ cup (125 mL) vegetable oil

PLUS

SEASONINGS — your choice — one from each grouping.

1.	2.	3.
½ tsp. (2-5 mL) basil	⅛-¼ tsp. (½-1 mL) chili	1 bay leaf
celery seed	powder	1-2 garlic cloves, peeled
marjoram	garlic powder	1-2 tsp. (5-10 mL)
oregano	pepper	horseradish
salt	ketchup	1 small onion
rosemary	soy sauce	
thyme	¼-½ cup (50-125 mL)	
paprika	chili sauce	

EQUALS

JUICY, SUPERBLY SUCCULENT, TENDER BEEF FIT FOR ONE AND ALL!!

ORIENTAL MARINADE

¼ cup	oil	50 mL
¼ cup	honey	50 mL
⅓ cup	dry sherry	75 mL
½ cup	soy sauce	125 mL
1	garlic glove, minced	1
1 tsp.	fresh, grated ginger root	5 mL
OR		
½ tsp.	dry ginger	2 mL
4	green onions, finely chopped	4

Thoroughly mix. Pour over beef.

TAHITIAN MARINADE

½ cup	soy sauce	125 mL
⅓ cup	horseradish	75 mL
¼ cup	wine vinegar	50 mL
¼ cup	lemon juice	50 mL
2 tbsp.	oil	30 mL
2 tbsp.	Worcestershire	30 mL
1 tbsp.	chopped parsley	15 mL
1 tbsp.	dry mustard	15 mL
2	garlic cloves, minced	2

Mix thoroughly. Pour over beef.

BARBECUING BEEF

Barbecuing is an all-time favorite 'family time' for most Canadians. Warm summer winds, fragrant with the aroma of freshly cut grass, colorful petunias, newly watered flower beds and the pungent smoke drifting by from the barbecue are all a call to enjoy. Enjoy good food, good fun and, most especially, good family times!

Beef with its great flavor and versatility is absolutely ideal for barbecuing. Everyone can relate to barbecued steaks . . . but wait, almost any cut of beef can be barbecued to perfection and at a very reasonable cost. Medium and less tender cuts of beef may require marinating . . . however, this provides your backyard cook with yet another opportunity to impress everyone with a different taste. Can you imagine the taste of beef that has been marinated in maple syrup? Aahhh . . . well then, you simply must give it a try. It's a long-standing family favorite and we're sure that it will become yours too!

BEST BEEF CUTS OR ROASTS
FOR THE BARBECUE

Planning a "get together"? Looking for a roast that will not only provide excellent eating but practically look after itself leaving you free to enjoy a warm summer afternoon with your gang? Look no further . . . *LEAN prime rib, rolled rib, rolled rump, sirloin tip and eye of the round await your culinary skills.

* Choose a fairly large roast, somewhere in the range of 5 lbs. (2.25 kg) and even larger depending on your crowd.

* Marinate if desired. Make sure the roast has some outer fat cover to protect it from drying out.

* Roasts should be securely tied and as compact and evenly shaped as possible.

* Baste with barbecue sauce or a marinade towards the last half hour of cooking.

ROTISSERIE OR 'SPIT' COOKING

Insert the rod lengthwise through the center of your roast. Tighten the holding forks and then check for balance. Your roast must turn smoothly and evenly with the rod.

The wonder of rotisserie cooking is that large cuts of beef will cook evenly and are self-basting.

A meat thermometer is recommended for outdoor cooking. It is difficult to judge when the meat is ready since cooking times, based on charcoal heat, can vary greatly.

Insert the thermometer in the thickest part of the roast.

Place a drip pan beneath your meat to catch drips and prevent flare-up. Position your coals around the pan.

Remove roast from the spit when thermometer reads about 5°F (2.5 °C) below desired degree of doneness. Allow the roast to set for 20 minutes, during which time it will continue to cook and it will carve more easily.

A 6 lb. (2.7 kg) roast will require about 2 to 2½ hours on the spit for rare.

KEEP *LEAN BEEF LEAN

Trim all visible fat from the meat on your plate. Careful trimming can decrease the calorie content by approximately half.

Make low-calorie substitutions in your recipes — for example, eliminate the oil, use yogurt in place of sour cream and substitute herbs and spices for butter and sauces.

Barbecuing on a grill allows any melted fat to drain off.

Cook stews, soups, and sauces a day in advance. Then refrigerate so the congealed fat can be easily removed before reheating.

BARBECUE-COOKING GUIDE

Initial Tenderness	Retail Cuts	How to Barbecue
Tender	Rib roast and steaks, wing, T-bone, strip loin, porterhouse, ground beef	Grill or cook on rotisserie to desired doneness. Use a medium-hot fire. Although a marinade is not necessary with tender cuts, you may wish to use one for additional flavor.
Medium Tender (group 1)	Round roasts, inside (top) & outside (bottom) round steak, sirloin tip roast and steak, rump roast	Marinating prior to cooking will increase tenderness. Grill or cook on rotisserie — preferably only to the medium-done stage.
Medium Tender (group 2)	Blade steak or roast, cross-rib steak or roast	Marinate or use commercial tenderizer before cooking. Grill steaks to medium stage. If roasts are not marinated wrap in foil and grill slowly to desired doneness. Remove foil for last 30 minutes.
Less Tender	Short ribs flank steak	Marinate or use commercial tenderizer before cooking. Grill short ribs slowly, brushing frequently with barbecue sauce. Grill flank steak quickly to medium-rare stage.

BARBECUE SECRET

Consider precooking your food before barbecuing. In many cases this will prevent food from drying out during a lengthy time over the coals. A good rule of thumb — allow at least 30 minutes of the total cooking time over the barbecue — time enough to achieve that unmistakable flavor and aroma of outdoor cooking.

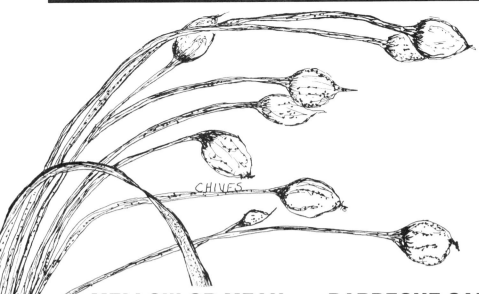

CHIVES

MELLOW OR MEAN . . . BARBECUE SAUCE

¼ cup	finely chopped onions or scallions	50 mL
¼ cup	finely chopped green pepper (mellow)	50 mL
OR		
¼ cup	finely chopped Jalapeño pepper (mean)	50 mL
¼ cup	finely chopped celery	50 mL
2 tbsp.	olive oil	30 mL
1 cup	tomato sauce	250 mL
1 cup	tomato paste	250 mL
¾ cup	ketchup	175 mL
⅓ cup	liquid honey	75 mL
¼ cup	vinegar or red wine	50 mL
1½ tsp.	soy sauce	7 mL
½	garlic clove, minced	½
1	bay leaf	1
½ tsp.	dry mustard	2 mL
¼ tsp.	chili powder	1 mL
1 tsp.	HP sauce	5 mL
¼ tsp.	Tabasco sauce (few drops)	1 mL
2 tbsp.	Worcestershire sauce	30 mL

- Sauté onions, pepper and celery in olive oil until tender. In a saucepan, combine vegetables with remaining ingredients. Mix thoroughly.
- Simmer for 2 hours stirring occasionally.
- Remove bay leaf.
- Sauce will remain usable for up to 1 month provided it is refrigerated. Reheat before using each time.

COOKING BEEF IN THE MICROWAVE

Beef is divided into three categories of tenderness. The cooking method and cooking time for beef in a microwave will vary with the tenderness of the cut being used.

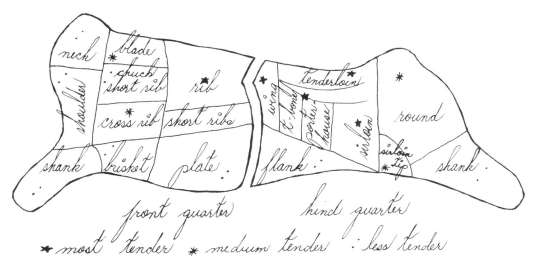

DO NOT SALT **BEFORE COOKING as salt dehydrates meat.

**Shielding or covering thin ends or bony tips of roasts with small pieces of foil is necessary to prevent overcooking in these areas.

MICROWAVE ROASTING FOR MOST TENDER CUTS
AT POWER: 50% (Medium)

- Brush browning agent on beef if darker color is desired. Insert meat thermometer. Place roast fat side down. Season to taste, excluding salt.
- Cover with waxed paper. Cook half the calculated time and rotate once during cooking.
- Turn roast over. Shield with foil when necessary. Remove any accumulated juices, set juices aside. This liquid diverts microwave energy from the roast and at the same time steams the roast. Replace waxed paper.
- Cook remaining time until desired internal temperature is reached.
- Loosely fold foil over roast. Do not wrap tightly. Let stand for 10-15 minutes.

MICROWAVE ROASTING FOR MEDIUM-TENDER CUTS

AT POWER: 50% FOR FIRST PART OF COOKING
AND 30% FOR LAST PART OF COOKING.

- Follow roasting method for most-tender cuts but cover with vented plastic wrap instead of wax paper.
- Calculate total cooking time and cook half the total time at 50% POWER (Medium.)
- Now increase the remaining time by half and continue cooking at 30% POWER. For example, if 60 minutes were required to cook the roast using only 50% POWER, then for medium beef roasts you would roast the first half for 30 minutes at 50% POWER, then 45 minutes at 30% power.

MICROWAVE ROASTING FOR LESS-TENDER CUTS

AT POWER: 50% (Medium).

- The liquid that is used in this method, called 'oven-braising', necessitates a slightly longer cooking time . . . 14-18 min./lb. (30-39 min./kg) for medium-done roasts.
- For better color, brush browning agent on beef.
- Place roast in casserole dish and add ¼ cup (50 mL) water, wine, broth or liquid of your choice.
- Cover tightly with lid or plastic wrap. If using plastic wrap fold back corner to allow vent for excess steam.
- Turn roast 2-3 times during cooking.
- Let stand covered for 10-15 minutes before carving.
- The juices from the roast may be served 'au naturel' or thickened for gravy.
- Roast will be slightly more tender if 30% POWER (Low) is used and time is increased by half.
- For maximum tenderness always carve roasts **ACROSS** the grain.
- All cooking times given are for beef placed in the microwave at refrigerated temperatures.

ROASTS IN THE MICROWAVE

When roasting in the microwave use a meat thermometer placed in the center of meat, being careful not to touch fat or bone.

Roasts continue to cook even when removed from microwave. It is therefore best to slightly undercook the roast.

DONENESS	INTERNAL TEMP.	TIME (using 50% POWER — Medium)
Rare	120°F (50°C)	9-12 min./lb (20-26 min./kg)
Medium	140°F (60°C)	10-14 min./lb. (22-30 min./kg)
Well-Done	160°F (70°C)	11-15 min./lb. (24-33 min./kg)

A roast cooked in the microwave does not attain the same color as one cooked in a conventional oven. Therefore, many cooks simply brush on one of the following browning agents . . . brown bouquet sauce diluted with water, Worcestershire sauce, barbecue sauce, soy sauce, concentrated beef bouillon or onion soup mix, which gives the roast greater eye appeal.

incredible brown mushrooms

**Our new *LEAN Canadian-produced BEEF is at the pinnacle of its ability to please you and your family when served with fresh vegetables which have been cooked in the microwave. Microwaving is the newest method of cooking vegetables and the most nutritional. Fast, waterless cooking ensures that nutrients are retained along with the color and texture of each vegetable. The vegetables literally cook in their own juices, thus preserving the integrity of their vitamin and mineral content.

*LEAN BEEF IS A NUTRIENT-DENSE FOOD!

Canadians today are very health oriented and their active, 'participaction' lifestyle demands nutrient-dense foods, foods that provide high amounts of nutrients in relation to their energy (calorie) content.

% Recommended daily nutrient intake* provided by a 3 oz. (90 g) serving of cooked lean beef.

Nutrient	%
Protein	47%
Riboflavin	15%
Thiamin	8%
Niacin	39%
Vitamin B6	21%
Vitamin B12	80%
Iron	41%
Zinc	53%
Phosphorous	28%
Calories	6%

* Recommended Nutrient Intake for Canadians, 1983. Health and Welfare Canada. Values based on adult male.

Beef is an extremely desirable food for everyone. Weight-conscious Canadians, children, adolescents, athletes, pregnant and lactating women will benefit from the many essential nutrients found in beef in a form that is readily absorbed by the body.

TODAY'S NEW BEEF — LEANER AND LIGHTER

CALORIE CONTENT
One cooked serving = 90 g (3 oz.) or equivalent as indicated

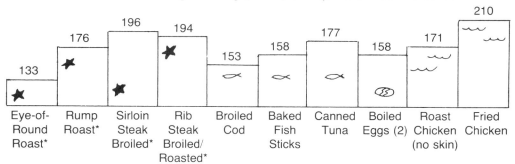

*Lean portion
Source: Jones, S.D.M. 1985 Chemical Composition of Selected Cooked Beef Steaks & Roasts,
J. Can. Diet. Assoc. 46:40
Canadian Nutrient File, 1983, Health & Welfare Canada

CHOLESTEROL CONTENT (mg)
One cooked serving = 90 g (3 oz.) or equivalent as indicated

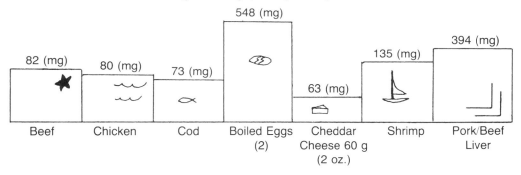

Source: Canadian Nutrient File, 1983, Health & Welfare Canada

FAT CONTENT (g)
One cooked serving = 90 g (3 oz.) or equivalent as indicated

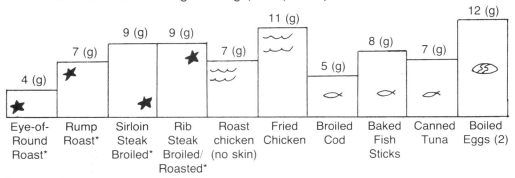

*Lean portion
Source: Jones, S.D.M. 1985 Chemical Composition of Selected Cooked Beef Steaks & Roasts,
J. Can. Diet. Assoc. 46:40
Canadian Nutrient File, 1983, Health & Welfare Canada

ENJOYING THE RIGHT WINE WITH BEEF

Beef is at its pleasurable best when served with a good wine. However, the choice of a particular wine depends less on the meat itself than on the ingredients used in the preparation of the dish.

Most beef dishes are enhanced by a red wine. The refined simplicity of a beef roast, unadorned with herbs or garlic, may well benefit from being served with a subtle, and delicately flavored French Bordeaux. Chambertin or Musigny, well-aged Côte de Nuits wines, would also allow the rich, robust flavor of beef to be savored.

Frequently, beef dishes containing tomatoes do not provide a very complementary background for the serving of red wines. The acidity found in tomatoes demands a young and fruity wine, one that can stand bold and hold its own. One might then consider a full-bodied white, from Italy, Frascati or Orvieto Secco. Closer to home and quite suitable for most beef and pasta dishes is a Gamay rosé from California or a red wine from the Niagara Peninsula, Marechal Foch.

Guests enjoying beef with a cream sauce such as Beef Stroganoff might well choose a dry, white Chardonnay or a Cabernet Sauvignon from the Okanagan valley in British Columbia.

Braised beef, with a variety of flavors present would be well supported by a young and robust wine from California, a Zinfandel perhaps, or a red from the Rhône Valley, such as Gigondas or Cornas. Not to be forgotten, from Italy, Barolo.

Personal preference is a most important factor in the choice of wine for your dinner. Whatever your choice — CHEERS!

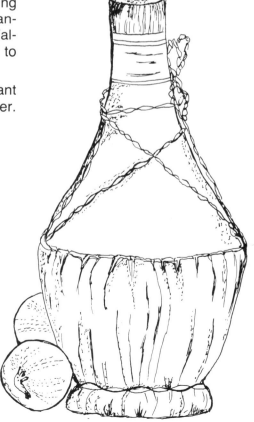

ROASTS

- **COOKING GUIDE**

- **A TREASURY OF ROASTS**

- **LEFTOVERS TO REMEMBER**

ANYWAY YOU SLICE IT —
*LEAN BEEF SOUNDS GOOD.

Do you remember those many family gatherings around which the serving of tender, succulent, juicy, *LEAN roast beef was the traditional Sunday favorite?

Do you remember the many ways in which you can enjoy leftover beef? Cold beef sandwiches with hot mustard sure sounds good for Tuesday's lunch, along with a couple of crispy, crunchy, pickles. Oh, and how about Deluxe Shepherd's Pie, page 33, for dinner on Wednesday!

ROAST BEEF COOKING GUIDE

ROAST	COOKING METHOD	DESCRIPTION
Rib Rump Sirloin tip Inside, Outside Eye of Round	Roast Roast or Oven Braise	Season roast with salt, pepper and garlic, if desired. Place roast in open roasting pan, fat side up. Do not add liquid or cover. Roast in pre-heated 325°F (160°C) oven for rib roast or slower oven 275°F (140°C) for rump, sirloin tip or round roasts.
Blade Cross rib	Oven Braise	Season roast. Place meat, fat side up, in roasting pan. Add ½" (1 cm) water to pan. Cover. Cook at 325°F (160°C) for 25 min./lb. (55 min./kg) adding liquid if necessary. Remove cover last 45 minutes.
Short rib Shoulder	Pot Roast	Brown roast in hot fat. Add approx. 1 cup (250 mL) liquid and seasonings. Cover. Simmer until tender — approx. 30 min./lb. (65 min./kg). Vegetables may be added during last ½ hour.

ROASTING TIMETABLE

Insert meat thermometer in center of roast for most accurate results.

At oven temperature of 325°F (160°C)
Rare — 20 min./lb. (45 min./kg)
Medium — 25 min./lb. (55 min./kg)
Well-done — 30 min./lb. (65-77 min./kg)

BE YOUR OWN BUTCHER

CUT A LITTLE — SAVE A LOT

**A large Sirloin Tip Roast will yield several different cuts suitable for varied dishes.

After removing the top layer of fat with a large boning knife, cut out the cap meat at the center of fat layer for kabobs (pages 46, 48, 49, 52, 54). Working parallel to the muscle fibers, cut the meat across the width, roughly in the center.

The thicker and meatier piece may be sliced into steaks or used, without tying, as a roast. The thinner piece, consists mainly of loosely connected muscle which in order to prevent falling apart during cooking, must be tied.

To tie a roast, you need only loop a string around one end of the meat and knot it, leaving a long end of string. Draw the long end across the meat and hold a short section flat. Loop the string around the meat and tie it to the short section. Repeat across the roast.

Slice the thicker piece of meat across the grain at ¾ to 1" (2 to 2.5 cm) intervals. Cut the cube end for kabobs.

In addition to steaks, a roast, and kabobs, a sirloin tip yields scraps which can be chopped or ground for hamburgers.

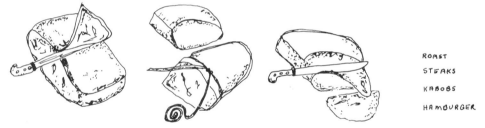

ROAST
STEAKS
KABOBS
HAMBURGER

**A Rib Roast provides a spectacular opportunity to extend your beef purchasing power.

Buy a large 10-13 pound (5-6½ kg) RIB roast from which you remove the entire rib-eye muscle and cut into steaks OR a small portion may be used for a small roast.

Rib bones can be frozen until enough ribs are available for a complete meal (see page 126).

The small feather bones underneath the rib bones are ideal for the preparation of soup or beef bouillon (page 148).

The removal of the cap provides beef that is perfect for cutting into strips for Stir-fries (pages 58, 60, 61, 62) and kabobs (pages 46, 48, 49, 52, 54).

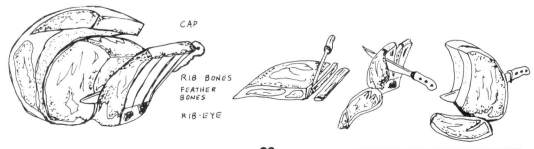

CAP

RIB BONES
FEATHER
BONES

RIB-EYE

ROAST BEEF WITH BÉARNAISE SAUCE

A large savory roast, medium rare, served with class and a touch of Béarnaise Sauce. Leftovers are delicious the following day, served cold and thinly sliced with a crisp salad. Don't forget 'Beef Diane' is great for cold leftover beef.

Wild Rice Gourmet, page 161, Tomato Aspic, page 157, and crusty French bread are perfect for this delicate and delectable serving of beef.

4 lbs.	*lean roast — inside — outside round with outside layer of fat	2 kg
dash	freshly ground pepper	dash

- Wipe meat with damp cloth and pat dry thoroughly. Preheat oven to 475°F (240°C).
- Cut away half of fat layer covering meat. Score remaining fat into diamonds with sharp knife, being careful not to cut into beef. Sprinkle all sides of meat generously with pepper, cover with foil and let stand for 10 minutes. Remove foil and insert meat thermometer into thickest part of roast. Place meat in roasting pan, fat side up. Place roasting pan on lowest rack in preheated oven.
- Roast 20 minutes, then reduce temperature to 400°F (200°C). Meat will be fully cooked in another 20-30 minutes. Roast to an internal temperature of 150°F (65.5°C) for medium rare.
- Remove the thermometer from meat, wrap tightly in foil and let rest 15 minutes. The juices from the roast will collect in the center during roasting time. Leaving it to sit for 15 minutes allows the juices to redistribute throughout the meat.
- Before slicing, quickly cut away external fat covering.
- Slice roast **across** the grain. Season with salt and pepper. Serve and pass the Béarnaise separately.

BÉARNAISE SAUCE

6 tbsp.	dry white wine	90 mL
¼ cup	tarragon vinegar	50 mL
2	shallots, skinned and minced	2
¼ tsp.	freshly ground pepper	1 mL
2 tsp.	mixed fresh tarragon and chervil sprigs	10 mL
1 cup	butter	250 mL
3	egg yolks	3
3 tbsp.	hot water	45 mL
1 tbsp.	finely chopped, fresh, tarragon leaves	15 mL
1½ tsp.	finely chopped, fresh, chervil leaves	7 mL
	salt	
	cayenne pepper	

BÉARNAISE SAUCE (CONT'D.)

- Combine shallots, pepper, herb sprigs, wine and vinegar in saucepan and bring to boil. Stir over medium heat until liquid is reduced to about 1 tbsp. (15 mL). Pour liquid through fine sieve, pressing on shallots and herbs to extract all the flavorful juices. Keep liquid warm.
- Place double-boiler top over double-boiler bottom containing hot, **not boiling** water. Add egg yolks and cook, beating constantly with wire whisk until slightly thickened.
- Add butter, about 2 tbsp. (30 mL) at a time, beating constantly with whisk, until butter is melted and mixture is thickened.
- Whisk in reduced wine mixture by teaspoon. Blend in chopped herbs. Season sauce with salt and cayenne and keep warm until served.
- Serves 6-8.

TANDOORI BEEF ROAST

Your passage to the exotic east, India, the land of the enormous elephants upon which, in times long past, rode the Maharajahs, splendorous and majestic.

So spectacular is this serving of rice pilaf, Tomato and Basil Salad page 156, and Tandoori beef roast that it might well have been waiting for the Maharajah and his entourage at the completion of their journey.

3-4 lbs.	*lean beef roast, blade, cross rib, or outside round	1.5-2 kg
1 cup	plain yogurt	250 mL
1	small onion, minced	1
2 tbsp.	lemon juice	30 mL
1½ tsp.	coriander, ground	7 mL
½ tsp.	cumin, ground	2 mL
½ tsp.	turmeric	2 mL
¼ tsp.	cardamom	1 mL
¼ tsp.	cayenne pepper	1 mL
1 tsp.	sugar	5 mL
1 tsp.	salt	5 mL
2 tsp.	paprika	10 mL
1	garlic clove, minced	1
3 tbsp.	tomato paste	45 mL
	liquid gravy coloring sauce	
¼ cup	flour	50 mL

- Pierce the roast in several places, top and bottom, with sharp knife.
- Combine yogurt, onion, lemon juice, coriander, cumin, turmeric, cardamom, cayenne, sugar, salt, paprika, garlic and tomato paste. Mix thoroughly.
- Pour the marinade over the roast; cover and refrigerate overnight or up to 24 hours. Turn roast several times. Drain marinade and reserve for the sauce.
- Brush diluted gravy browning sauce on all sides of roast. Place roast on a microwave roasting rack. Cover with waxed paper.
- At 50% POWER (Medium) in microwave allow: approximately 12 minutes per lb. (26 minutes per kg) for rare and approximately 13 minutes per lb. (28 minutes per kg) for medium.

- Cook half the total time. Turn roast over. Drain accumulated juices and save for the sauce.
- Shield outside edges and along bone with small pieces of foil. Recover with wax paper and cook remaining time.
- Remove from microwave; cover loosely with foil and let stand 15 minutes.

SAUCE

Blend flour and ½ tsp. (2 mL) liquid browning agent with reserved marinade. Add cooking juices. Cook at 100% POWER (High) for 3 minutes. Stir, continue cooking for 2 minutes. Pass sauce when serving thin slices of beef roast. Serves 8-10.

POLYNESIAN POT ROAST

An early morning promise of parslied potatoes, grilled tomatoes, warm, whole-wheat dinner rolls and . . . Polynesian pot roast is enough to make even a Monday workday seem not so bad!

3 lbs.	*beef chuck roast	1.5 kg
¼ cup	all-purpose flour	50 mL
2 tbsp.	butter	30 mL
14 oz.	can pineapple slices	398 mL
¼ cup	soy sauce	50 mL
4 tbsp.	lemon juice	60 mL
3 tbsp.	brown sugar	45 mL
½ tsp.	dried basil	2 mL
1	garlic clove, minced	1
¼ cup	water	50 mL
2 tbsp.	cornstarch	30 mL

- Trim any excess fat from meat and coat with flour.
- In Dutch oven, brown meat on all sides in butter. Combine drained pineapple juice, brown sugar, basil and garlic. Pour over roast in Dutch oven. Roast at 350°F (180°C) for 2 hours or until meat is tender. Baste occasionally with soy mixture. During last 10 minutes of roasting, top with pineapple slices.
- Transfer roast and pineapple to platter, keep warm. Pour pan juices into measuring cup, skim off fat. Add water to juices to make 2 cups (500 mL) and return to pan.
- Mix ½ cup (50 mL) water with cornstarch and add a small amount of hot pan juices. Stir thoroughly. Stir cornstarch mixture into pan juices. Stir until thickened and bubbly. Serve the sauce with roast.
- Serves 6.

BAYOU-BARBECUED, POT-ROAST DINNER

Lush, resplendent foliage lends an unimaginable beauty to bayous left isolated by a change in the course of a river during the flood season. Steamy, summer days everywhere bring to mind the pleasures of a barbecue.

You absolutely must give this pot roast a try! The accompanying sauce lends itself to the recipe by gently marinating the roast even while cooking. This 'one-step' dinner leaves plenty of time to enjoy summer sounds and the warmth of the sun.

4 lbs.	*lean blade or cross-rib roast	2 kg
dash	salt and pepper	dash
1 cup	ketchup	250 mL
3 tbsp.	flour	45 mL
2 tbsp.	Worcestershire sauce	30 mL
2 tbsp.	soy sauce	30 mL
¼ cup	red wine	50 mL
1½ tbsp.	vinegar	22 mL
1 tbsp.	brown sugar	15 mL
1 tsp.	dry mustard	5 mL
3	potatoes, peeled and quartered	3
2	medium onions, sliced	2
3	green peppers, seeded and quartered	3
3	carrots, cut in ½'' (1-2 cm) slices	3
2 stalks	celery, cut in ½'' (1-2 cm) slices	2 stalks

- Slowly brown roast on both sides, on a grill, over hot coals. Season with salt and pepper to taste.
- Mix together ketchup, flour, Worcestershire sauce, soy sauce, red wine, vinegar, brown sugar, mustard, 1 tsp. (5 mL) salt and a dash of pepper.
- Place browned meat in the center of a 2 foot (60 cm) length of heavy-duty foil. Cover with half of the ketchup sauce. Arrange vegetables on top and add remaining sauce. Bring both long ends of foil together, rolling excess into a flat ridge across the top. Turn sides up and seal securely.
- Place on grill with double thickness on bottom. Bake over slow coals about 2-2½ hours or until meat is tender. Check by unfolding a small section of foil on top and piercing meat with a long fork, being careful not to let sauce run out.
- When done, carefully remove vegetables to a warm serving dish and place meat on a warm platter. Use sauce as a gravy when serving.
- Serves 8-10.

PALERMO POT ROAST

Seasoned with gusto, this pot roast is flavorful, melt-in-your-mouth tender.

Long-grain or wild rice, fresh asparagus tips and warmed dinner rolls provide a very special dinner for a cold wintery evening!

5 lbs.	*lean boned beef rump roast	2.5 kg
2	garlic cloves, minced	2
2½ tsp.	salt	12 mL
3 tbsp.	vegetable oil	45 mL
3	onions, sliced	3
5 tsp.	chili powder	25 mL
1 tsp.	cumin	5 mL
½ tsp.	ground coriander	2 mL
⅔ cup	tomato paste	150 mL
1	beef bouillon cube	1
19 oz.	can tomatoes	540 mL

- Early in the day, mash garlic with 2 tsp. (10 mL) salt. Make slashes in rump roast and fill them with garlic mixture. Cover and return to refrigerator.
- Heat oil in very large saucepan or Dutch oven and brown rump evenly on all sides. Add onions, sauté until golden.
- Add ½ tsp. (2 mL) salt, chili powder, cumin, coriander, tomato paste and beef bouillon cube. Add liquid drained from tomatoes plus enough water to make 1¼ cups (300 mL). Simmer, covered for 2½ hours or until almost tender. Add tomatoes and simmer about 15 minutes more, until rump is tender.
- Transfer roast to serving platter. Top with some gravy and pass the rest while serving.
- Serves 8-10.

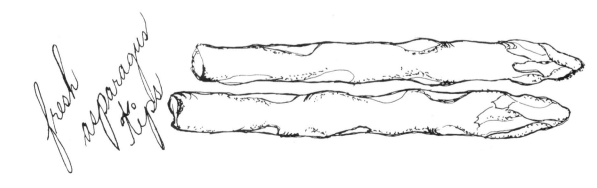

fresh asparagus tips

PEPPER RIB EYE OF BEEF

A hot, peppery marinade, coupled with a very lean cut of beef is enough to make anyone look forward to tonight's dinner, more so when you mention that, for a rapid change of pace, your own homemade Horseradish Sauce will be available to those daring enough to try it.

4 lbs.	*lean rib eye roast	2 kg
⅓ cup	whole black peppercorns, coarsely ground	75 mL
½ tsp.	ground cardamom seed	2 mL
½ tsp.	ground cloves	2 mL
2 tsp.	Dijon-style mustard	10 mL
1 tbsp.	tomato paste	15 mL
1 tsp.	paprika	5 mL
½ tsp.	garlic salt	2 mL
1 cup	soy sauce	250 mL
¾ cup	red wine vinegar	175 mL

- Place beef in 9" x 13" (22 x 33 cm) baking dish. Combine pepper, cardamom seed and cloves. Firmly press pepper mixture into beef. Combine mustard, tomato paste, paprika and garlic salt in small bowl. Stir in soy sauce and vinegar. Pour marinade over beef. Cover and refrigerate overnight, basting occasionally.
- Remove beef from refrigerator and let stand at room temperature for 1 hour.
- Preheat oven to 300°F (150°C). Remove beef from marinade and wrap tightly in heavy-duty foil. Roast to desired doneness, about 2 hours for medium rare.

HORSERADISH SAUCE

1 cup	sour cream	250 mL
1 tbsp.	grated, drained horseradish	15 mL
1 tbsp.	Dijon-style mustard	15 mL
1 tsp.	lemon juice	5 mL
dash	salt	dash
dash	pepper	dash

- Combine ingredients and mix thoroughly.
- Serves 8.

BEEF DIANE

What a super beef preparation Beef Diane is. A fantastic recipe for utilizing, with a touch of pizzazz, leftover cold beef!

8-12	slices *lean rare roast beef	8-12
3 tbsp.	butter	45 mL
1 tbsp.	red wine or brandy	15 mL
8	fresh mushrooms, sliced	8
1 tbsp.	fresh lemon juice	15 mL
3 tbsp.	gravy**	45 mL
1 tbsp.	Worcestershire sauce	15 mL
3 tbsp.	red wine or brandy	45 mL
dash	salt	dash
dash	pepper	dash

- In heavy skillet, heat thinly sliced beef slices slowly in butter. Place on heated platter.
- Add 1 tbsp. (15 mL) wine or brandy to skillet and brown mushrooms. Add remaining ingredients and heat until bubbling.
- Pour hot sauce over beef slices.
- Serves 4-6.

**If you don't have gravy available, dissolve 1 beef bouillon cube in ¼ cup (50 mL) boiling water. Use 3 tbsp. (45 mL) of this beef stock in place of gravy.

OLD-TIME DOUBLE-CRUST MEAT PIE

A perfect Monday morning recipe calling for leftover roast beef and gravy. Wasn't it grand to enjoy the whole family gathering on Sunday? Good food and raucous laughter — the type of laughter generated by love and 'insider information'.

PASTRY

⅔ cup	shortening	150 mL
2 tbsp.	butter	30 mL
2¼ cups	flour	550 mL
1 tsp.	salt	5 mL
2½ tbsp.	ice cold water	35 mL

FILLING

2	medium potatoes	2
4 cups	leftover roast beef	1 L
1 cup	leftover gravy	250 mL
1	small onion	1
¼	green pepper, chopped	¼
1	beef bouillon cube	1
½ tsp.	salt	2 mL
¼ tsp.	freshly ground pepper	1 mL
dash	garlic salt	dash

- Cut shortening and butter into flour and salt until the size of peas. Sprinkle water over mixture, while tossing with a fork, until all the flour is dampened.
- Press into ball between palms. Roll out half to fit a deep 9" x 2" (22 x 5 cm) pie plate and line plate. Roll out other half.
- After scrubbing potatoes clean, cook in 1 cup (250 mL) water until they are slightly tender. DO NOT OVERCOOK — potatoes should not be too soft. When potatoes are cooked save the liquid, and peel and dice them into ½" (1 cm) cubes.
- While potatoes are cooking, grind leftover beef to measure 4 cups (1 L) of beef. Gradually grind onion at the same time, so that onion is mixed throughout the meat. Add leftover gravy and green peppers.
- Add potatoes, potato water, beef bouillon cube and salt, pepper and garlic salt to meat mixture. Mix well and stir over medium heat until mixture just begins to boil. If it becomes too thick add a little more water. It should be just wet enough to pour.
- Pour hot meat filling into lined pie plate. Cover with top crust, score crust to allow moisture to escape and crimp edges carefully.
- To glaze, brush with beaten egg yolk or white. Bake at 450°F (230°C) for 15 minutes then reduce heat to 350°F (180°C) for another 20 minutes or until filling begins to bubble through holes in crust and crust turns a golden brown.
- Serves 4-6.

Gourmet Stuffed Steak with Onion Stuffing, page 43

DELUXE SHEPHERD'S PIE

The origin of Shepherd's pie is, at best, uncertain. However, one could probably assume that its development lay within the imagination of a frugal homemaker with a highly developed sense of flair and a cultivated palate. How else could one explain the universality and longevity of this family favorite?

ONE OF THE BEST RECIPES FOR LEFTOVER ROAST BEEF, snuggled into a pastry shell, generously covered with creamy, fluffy potatoes baked golden brown and served piping hot!

PASTRY

⅓ cup	shortening	75 mL
2 tbsp.	butter	30 mL
1¼ cups	pastry flour, stirred but unsifted	300 mL
½ tsp.	salt	2 mL
1 tbsp.	cold water	15 mL

FILLING

2 cups	*lean leftover roast beef, ground or finely chopped	500 mL
1	small onion, chopped	1
10 oz.	can vegetable soup, undiluted	284 mL
1¾ cups	packed, unseasoned mashed potatoes	425 mL
	melted butter for glaze	

- Cook potatoes in boiling salted water, covered, until tender.
- Make the pastry by cutting the shortening and butter into the flour and salt until the size of peas. Sprinkle water over mixture, while tossing with a fork, until all flour is dampened. Press into a ball and roll out on well-floured board to fit a deep pie plate, 9" x 2" (22 x 5 cm).
- Combine the ground or chopped lean beef and onion with the undiluted soup. Drain and mash potatoes until perfectly smooth.
- Turn meat mixture into pastry-lined pie plate. Smooth top.
- Carefully cover with spoonfuls of mashed potatoes and spread with a fork. Brush top with melted butter. Bake at 400°F (200°C) for 25 minutes. Reduce heat to 350°F (180°C) and bake for an additional 10 minutes.
- Provides 6 scrumptious servings.

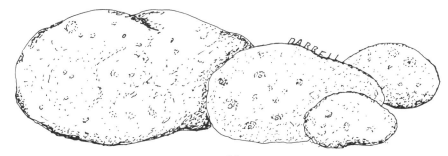

MEAT STORAGE — THE SAFE WAY

- Meat must be refrigerated as quickly as possible after purchase.
- FRESH MEAT — loosen store wrappings and rewrap loosely in waxed paper.
- Check processing/packaging date on meat label . . . buy only 'fresh packed.' Ground or cubed beef, or variety meat such as liver or kidney should be cooked within 24 hours of purchase.
- FROZEN MEAT should be left wrapped in the refrigerator to thaw rather than at room temperature.
- Cook meat as soon as it is thawed. NEVER refreeze thawed meat, unless it has been cooked.

STORAGE TIPS FOR GROUND BEEF

- Ground beef may be stored for up to 2 days in refrigerator.
- It is best to thaw ground beef in refrigerator to ensure optimum quality and safety.
- Avoid refreezing thawed beef unless there are ice crystals still present.
- If ground beef must be refrozen, it should be cooked first, then frozen.
- COOKED ground beef dishes may be frozen for 2-3 months if well-wrapped.
- FRESH ground beef, if properly packaged, can be frozen and stored for 3 to 6 months.

beef to peppers

STEAKS

- **SPECIAL OCCASION**

- **SPECIAL OCCASION FLAVOR — BUDGET PRICES**

PEPPERCORNS IN TENDERLOIN

Tenderloin *LEAN beef is one of the finest and tastiest cuts of beef. Carefully cooked it becomes a treasure to share on those special occasions.

The explosion of flavor in this dish is the blending of equal parts of green, black and white peppercorns and whole allspice in a peppermill for coarse grinding and sprinkling on the tenderloin. Simplicity . . . is spectacular!!

3-4 lbs.	*lean beef tenderloin, fat totally trimmed away	1.5-2 kg
3 tbsp.	Dijon-style mustard	45 mL
1½ tbsp.	green peppercorns, (packed in water) drained	22 mL
3 tbsp.	peppercorn blend equal amounts of green, black, white, peppercorns and allspice . . . coarsely ground in peppermill	45 mL
1 tbsp.	lemon peel, dried	15 mL
8	fresh, large sage leaves	8
2 tbsp.	unsalted butter, at room temperature	30 mL
dash	salt	dash
4	bay leaves	4

- Preheat oven to 425°F (220°C).
- Using a sharp knife, make a cut lengthwise down the center of the tenderloin through ⅔ of the thickness. Spread the meat open and flatten slightly with palm of hands and thumbs.
- Spread mustard in a thin layer over the opened tenderloin. Sprinkle the green peppercorns over evenly and lightly press into the meat with your hands. Shake 1 tbsp. (15 mL) of the peppercorn blend on top of green peppercorns. Sprinkle lemon peel over peppercorns. Place the sage leaves lengthwise down the center.
- Close the tenderloin and tie securely with string in several places. Rub the outside of the tenderloin first with butter and then with the remaining peppercorn. Sprinkle with salt to taste.
- Place, seam down, in a shallow roasting pan, slipping bay leaves under the strings on top of the meat.
- Roast the beef for 45-50 minutes for rare meat. Let stand for 10 minutes before carving. Spoon 'jus au naturel' over beef slices.
- Serves 6-8 and are they in for a treat! Robust beef, a bottle of your favorite wine, Potato Petals, page 160, and Honey-Glazed Shallots with Mint, page 158, will leave your palate wondering why it never felt this good before!

FILLET OF BEEF en FRANÇAISE

Delicious . . . delicious . . . and for good measure, once more with feeling, 'Fillet of Beef en Française' is delicious. Five fortunate guests could grace your table while you offer beef fillet, Potato Petals, page 160, Tomatoes with Horse-radish Sauce, page 156, fresh asparagus and, of course, French bread!

3 lbs.	*lean fillet of beef	1.5 kg
3 oz.	blanched almonds	85 g
2 oz.	smooth liver pâté	55 g
2 tbsp.	cognac	30 mL
3 tbsp.	oil	45 mL
dash	salt	dash
dash	freshly ground pepper	dash
	Sour Cream Pastry to enclose beef, (page 159)	
1	egg, beaten	1

- Grind almonds as finely as you can in a blender. Mix almonds with pâté and cognac.
- Make an incision down the center of fillet and fill with almond mixture. Skewer closed.
- In a large skillet heat oil and brown fillet on all sides — the time cooked depends on how rare you like your meat since it won't cook much inside the pastry. Season to taste.
- Roll out pastry ¼" (½ cm) thick, then enclose meat in it. Make sure all pastry edges are pinched closed. Brush top and sides with beaten egg and bake uncovered in a 400°F (200°C) oven for 30 minutes or until pastry is golden.
- Slice at the table.
- Serves 6.

BEEF WELLINGTON

Truly spectacular, worthy of an occasion when the people you most care about gather together and enjoy a dinner that will become a cherished memory. Gleaming cutlery, sparkling crystal catching a burst of light from a gently wavering candle, crisp, blue-white linen and for a centerpiece, a bowl containing a single, majestic red rose. This setting provides an ambience that is intimate and memorable.

4 lbs.	*lean fillet of beef	2 kg
¾ cup	Burgundy	175 mL
¾ cup	dry sherry	175 mL
2	bay leaves	2
1	onion, quartered	1
2 cups	all-purpose flour	500 mL
½ tsp.	salt	2 mL
⅔ cup	shortening	150 mL
⅓-½ cup	cold water	75-125 mL
½ cup	liver pâté	125 mL
1	egg, beaten	1
1½ cups	cold water	375 mL
2 tsp.	instant bouillon granules	10 mL
½ cup	cold water	125 mL
¼ cup	all-purpose flour	50mL
⅓ cup	burgundy	75 mL
½ tsp.	dried basil, crushed	2 mL
	salt	
	pepper	

- To make marinade, combine burgundy, sherry, bay leaves and onion. Place meat in clear plastic bag; set in deep bowl. Pour marinade over meat; close. Refrigerate overnight; turning bag occasionally.
- Place beef on rack in shallow roasting pan. Insert meat thermometer. Roast beef at 425°F (220°C) until thermometer registers 270°F (135°C), about 50 minutes. Remove from pan, cool. Reserve drippings.
- Mix flour and salt. With fork, cut in shortening until size of small peas. Add ⅓-½ cup (75-125 mL) cold water, 1 tbsp. (15 mL) at a time, tossing with fork until all flour is moistened. Form into ball and chill for 30 minutes.
- On lightly floured surface, roll dough into rectangle approximately 14" x 12" (35 x 30 cm). Spread pâté to within ½" (1.5 cm) of edge.
- Place roast in center and overlap long edges. Brush on egg and seal. Remove excess pastry from ends. Place on greased baking sheet, seam side down. Reroll trimmings and make fanciful cutouts. Place on meat and brush remaining egg over pastry. Bake at 425°F (220°C) for 35 minutes (Meat will be rare).

BEEF WELLINGTON (CONT'D.)

- Heat and stir reserved drippings with 1½ cups (375 mL) water and bouillon granules until dissolved. Mix ½ cup (125 mL) cold water with ¼ cup (50 mL) flour; stir into hot mixture with Burgundy and basil. Cook and stir until bubbly. Season with salt and pepper to taste. Pass for individual preference at the dinner table.
- Serves 12.

STEAK DIANE

Steak Diane, — easy and so very tasty. Beef tenderloin is probably the most succulent, most flavorful and most tender cut of beef, — one which surely would delight your resident epicures.

4	*lean beef tenderloin steaks (4-6 oz. [125-170 g])	4
½ tsp.	salt	2 mL
⅛ tsp.	freshly ground pepper	0.5 mL
4 tbsp.	butter, divided	60 mL
1½ tbsp.	Dijon-style mustard	22 mL
2 tsp.	Worcestershire sauce, divided	10 mL
2 cups	thinly sliced mushrooms	500 mL
2 tbsp.	minced shallots	30 mL
3 tbsp.	chopped chives	45 mL
¼ cup	brandy	50 mL
½ cup	Beef Bouillon (page 148)	125 mL

SHALLOTS & STEAK

- Place tenderloin steak between waxed paper and press with your hand until ¼" (½ cm) thick.
- Rub steaks in salt and pepper.
- In large skillet melt 1 tbsp. (15 mL) butter. Add steaks and brown about 1 minute each side; remove steak to a platter. Spread both sides of steak with mustard and sprinkle with 1 tsp. (5 mL) Worcestershire; set aside.
- In same skillet, melt remaining butter. Add mushrooms, shallots and chives; sauté for 2 minutes. Add brandy and flame. Stir in bouillon and remaining Worcestershire. Cook and stir until hot.
- Return steaks to skillet and reheat for 2 minutes. Sprinkle with parsley, if desired.
- Serves 4.

MARINATED CHUCK STEAK

Marinated chuck steak is excellent served with Wild Rice Gourmet, page 161. Grilled tomatoes and green peas offer, not only a most pleasant visual presentation, but a delicate balance to your meal.

Coffee and dessert . . . a fresh fruit compote, will understandably have your family wondering how you manage to accomplish everything!

1 lb.	*lean boneless chuck steak	500 g
2 tbsp.	teriyaki sauce	30 mL
2 tsp.	honey	10 mL
2 tsp.	red wine	10 mL
dash	ground ginger	dash
1 tsp.	scallion, slivered	5 mL

- Combine teriyaki sauce, honey, wine and ginger; pour marinade over the beef. Cover and refrigerate for about 1 to 4 hours, turning occasionally. Don't forget to pierce the steak with a fork, top and bottom, so that the marinade will quietly seep through the entire cut for maximum tenderness and flavor.
- Remove steak from marinade and place in oven to broil 5 minutes on each side or until cooked to desired doneness.
- Slice steak **across the grain** and place on a serving platter. Garnish with slivered scallions.
- Marinated Chuck Steak is also great on the barbecue. Try it!
- Serves 2.

FIESTA FILET MIGNON

Beef fillets wrapped individually to 'greedily' capture all the flavor possible for the imminent arrival of Grandpa and Grandma.

Luxuriously tender fillets of beef are most befitting this occasion for they set the tone of timeless satisfaction with good company, story telling and memories. Enjoy a quality, young Bordeaux wine, such as Médoc, and linger awhile.

4	*lean beef fillets, 1'' (2.5 cm) thick	4
½	Spanish onion, chopped	½
4	chicken livers, chopped	4
½ cup	butter	125 mL
½ cup	dry red wine	125 mL
½ tsp.	salt	2 mL
4 tsp.	chopped, fresh parsley	20 mL
24	toasted almonds	24

- Broil fillets to taste and set aside.
- Cook onion and liver in butter until tender, add wine and salt and simmer until mixture thickens.

- Using heavy aluminum foil, shape 4 pieces into the form of a small saucer. Pour sauce into each piece of foil, using half the mixture. Add the steaks and pour on the rest of sauce.
- Divide parsley and almonds among the 4 servings and close them tightly with additional aluminum foil. Make sure the edges are completely sealed.
- Cook in a 500°F (260°C) oven for about 5 minutes and serve in foil.
- Serves 4.

CARPETBAGGER STEAK

One of the many good things that has come to us from the land down under and her spirited people — the indefatigable 'Aussies'. What a perfect blending of foods common to this continent! Shiraz, an Australian red wine, makes this steak rendition something to remember.

4 steaks	*lean beef tenderloin fillets	4 steaks
8	canned oysters	8
¼ tsp.	salt	1 mL
dash	freshly ground pepper	dash
dash	Tabasco sauce	dash
2 tbsp.	butter	30 mL
1 tbsp.	vegetable oil	15 mL
4 tbsp.	melted butter (optional)	60 mL
1 tbsp.	finely chopped parsley (optional)	15 mL

- Each steak must have a pocket in which to place the oysters. If your super-market has an in-store butcher service, chances are that they will cut your meat.
- If not, place the steaks on a chopping board. With a long sharp knife, cut a horizontal slit about 2" (5 cm) wide and 2½-3" (6-8 cm) deep into the side of the steak. **DO NOT** cut through to the other side.
- Sprinkle the oysters with salt, pepper and Tabasco sauce. Place 2 oysters in each steak. Close the pocket with skewers or sew them shut, using a large needle and cotton thread.
- Pat the steaks completely dry with paper towelling and sprinkle to taste with pepper.
- In a heavy skillet, melt the butter with vegetable oil. Add steaks and brown quickly for 1 or 2 minutes on each side, turning steaks with tongs to avoid puncturing meat.
- Reduce the heat to moderate and sauté the steaks to desired doneness — 8 minutes if you like rare beef, 10 minutes if you prefer medium rare. Turn the steaks frequently so that the pepper does not form a crust.
- Serve the steaks immediately with melted butter combined with chopped parsley poured over top.
- Serves 4.

CARNE ASADA ROASTED MEAT

A sparkling cold brew, along with Alberta Baked Beans, page 162 and Tomato Aspic, page 157, is the touch of genius needed for this spicy Spanish beef rendition. No one . . . absolutely no one, will leave your dinner table for many hours. So relax, have fun, enjoy and make sure the rooster is safely gagged and tucked away so that you can linger in bed tomorrow morning!

4	*lean tenderloin steaks (about 3 lbs. [1.5 kg] in total)	4
⅓ cup	fresh lime juice	75 mL
3	garlic cloves, minced	3
2 tbsp.	vegetable oil	30 mL
2 tbsp.	lemon juice	30 mL
½ tsp.	dried red pepper flakes	2 mL
dash	salt	dash
dash	freshly ground pepper	dash
6	pita bread	6
1 jar	Salsa Sauce, warmed	1 jar

- Place steaks in a shallow glass casserole dish. Sprinkle with lime juice, garlic, oil, lemon juice and red pepper flakes. Set aside at room temperature for 1 hour.
- Brush both sides of steak with oil and season with salt and pepper to taste.
- Barbecue steaks to desired doneness.
- Thinly slice the steaks **across** the grain and serve in Pita pockets with warmed Salsa Sauce as a topping. WOW!
- Serves 5-6.

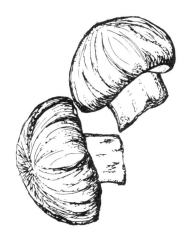

GOURMET STUFFED STEAK

| 4 steaks | *lean rib-eye, porterhouse, strip loin or tenderloin steaks, 1¼'' (3 cm) thick | 4 steaks |

Fill your steak with either the onion or shrimp stuffing.
- Cut a deep pocket in the side of each steak. Stuff pockets with onion or shrimp mixture and skewer closed.
- Barbecue steak over medium hot coals for approximately 20 minutes or until desired doneness, turning once and brushing the onion-stuffed steaks with basting sauce. Great for oven broiling also.
- Serves 4-8.
- See photograph, page 32.

SHRIMP STUFFING

2 tbsp.	butter	30 mL
¼ cup	chopped green onion	50 mL
½ cup	chopped celery	125 mL
2 tbsp.	sliced olives	30 mL
1 cup	canned baby shrimp	250 mL
1 tbsp.	lemon juice	15 mL
1 tbsp.	white wine	15 mL
to taste	salt	to taste
to taste	pepper	to taste
to taste	savory	to taste
to taste	parsley	to taste

ONION STUFFING

2 tbsp.	butter	30 mL
½ cup	chopped onion	125 mL
½ cup	chopped celery	125 mL
1 tsp.	chopped pimiento	5 mL
1	garlic clove, finely chopped	1
dash	salt	dash
dash	pepper	dash

- For either stuffing, sauté the vegetables in butter until tender-crisp. Add remaining ingredients. Heat thoroughly.

BASTING SAUCE — for onion-stuffed steak

| ¼ cup | dry red wine | 50 mL |
| 2 tbsp. | soy sauce | 30 mL |

- Mix thoroughly.

BEEF TENDERLOIN FOR TWOGETHERNESS

Serve tenderloin with flat noodles, lightly coated with butter and seasoned with salt and pepper and a bottle of wine from Southern France, such as, Coteaux du Languedoc. Carrots, colorful, long and slender, asparagus, lightly tossed in a sauce of ½ tsp. (2 mL) butter, 1 tsp. (5 mL) vinegar and a pinch of sugar will add a touch of 'gourmet' to your dinner. And for dessert . . . MISSISSIPPI MUD', page 168.

¾ lb.	*lean beef tenderloin, cut into 6 strips	0.4 kg
dash	salt	dash
dash	pepper	dash
4 slices	bacon, cut into thick strips	4 slices
¼ cup	pearl onions	50 mL
½ lb.	mushrooms, quartered	250 g
½ cup	red wine	125 mL
1 cup	brown gravy	250 mL

- In a large skillet, heat a bit of oil. Salt and pepper meat on both sides of strips and sauté to medium rare, approximately 4 minutes. Remove meat from skillet and replace oil with butter.
- Add bacon, onion and mushrooms. Sauté until lightly browned.
- Add red wine and simmer to reduce the liquid to half. Add the gravy and let simmer for 4 minutes.

BROWN GRAVY

2	beef bouillon cubes	2
1 cup	boiling water	250 mL
1 tsp.	flour	5 mL
1 tsp.	butter	5 mL

- Dissolve beef bouillon in boiling water. In a saucepan, melt butter and add flour. Slowly add ¾ cup (175 mL) beef bouillon juices to flour mixture in saucepan. Stir constantly until smooth, adding a pinch of salt and pepper.
- Just before serving, place the meat and drippings into the sauce and reheat. Taste and adjust seasoning if necessary.
- Just right for a dinner for you and your partner in crime.

BEEF STROGANOFF

Probably found on more menus throughout the world than any other meat dish, and for good reason! Exquisitely subtle taste begging the company of a delightful Spanish Rioja wine. Beef Stroganoff, a classic for those who appreciate the finest and the best!

1½ lbs.	*lean beef tenderloin, cut in ⅜'' x ⅜'' (1 cm x 1 cm) thick strips	750 g
1 tbsp.	vegetable oil	15 mL
3 tbsp.	butter	45 mL
1	onion, small, finely chopped	1
6-7 oz.	mushrooms, finely chopped	170-200 g
dash	salt	dash
dash	freshly ground pepper	dash
2-3 tsp.	prepared mustard	10-15 mL
1⅓ cup	sour cream	325 mL
1½ tsp.	beef bouillon (page 148)	7 mL
1 tbsp.	fresh lemon juice	15 mL

- In a 12'' (30 cm) skillet over medium heat, in oil, cook beef strips until meat is well browned on both sides, about 10 minutes. As each batch of beef is cooked remove to platter.
- When all meat is cooked, add remaining butter to skillet. Add onion, mushrooms, salt and pepper and cook, stirring, until onions are translucent and mushrooms are soft.
- Stir in mustard and cook briefly. Add a few drops of water and scrape up browned bits from bottom of pan. Add sour cream. Stir in beef bouillon and lemon juice.
- Season meat with salt and pepper; stir into sauce, along with any juices that may have settled on the platter.
- Heat slowly over medium heat, stirring constantly — do not cook beef beyond this point or it may become tough.
- Serve immediately with fettuccini, and the ultimate in salads . . . a CAESAR, page 150. Don't forget to try 'sippets!' page 155.
- Serves 4.

SKEWERED SPICY BEEF

When first we tried skewered spicy beef we did so with several other fortunate people. Today, however, when this beef recipe is in the making a total news blackout occurs and then there is more to enjoy. Conspiracy leads to skewered spicy beef being a great 'twogetherness' meal.

1 lb.	*lean boneless sirloin steak	500 g
1½ tbsp.	grated fresh ginger root	22 mL
1	large garlic clove, grated	1
4	green onions, grated	4
½ cup	soy sauce	125 mL
2 tbsp.	dry sherry	30 mL
1 tbsp.	lime juice	15 mL
2 drops	Tabasco sauce	2 drops
1 tbsp.	sesame oil	15 mL
2 tsp.	sugar	10 mL
½ tsp.	dry mustard	2 mL
1	jalapeño pepper, finely chopped	1
25 approx.	wooden skewers	25 approx.

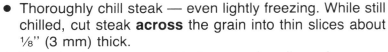

- Thoroughly chill steak — even lightly freezing. While still chilled, cut steak **across** the grain into thin slices about ⅛'' (3 mm) thick.
- To a food processor add ginger and garlic and process until finely chopped. Add onions; mix thoroughly. Add soy sauce, sherry, lime juice, Tabasco, oil, sugar, dry mustard and jalapeño pepper. Mix thoroughly.
- Add mixture to meat, stirring until coated. Cover and set aside at room temperature for 30 minutes. Refrigerate at this time if not ready to barbecue.
- Soak skewers in water for at least ½ hour. Thread marinated meat onto skewers, much as you would hand sew a rough seam. Again, if not using immediately, pour marinade over beef, cover and refrigerate.
- Barbecue skewered beef over grills for 1 to 2 minutes on each side or until desired doneness. Baste with any remaining marinade.
- Serves 8 appetizer servings or "TWOgetherness", entrées.
- See photograph, page 48.

HUNGARIAN PEPPER STEAK SERVED WITH
NOODLES CARAWAY

Spicy pepper steak and noodles caraway; if that isn't enough, then for good measure add a dollop or two of sour cream. A clean, bright salad dressing of oil and vinegar along with fresh French bread and no one will want to leave the dinner table. Especially if they know that a cold and light lime sherbet will be served along with coffee.

1½ lbs.	*lean top sirloin or chuck, well-trimmed and cut diagonally into ½'' (1 cm) slices	750 g
	flour	
	salt	
2 tbsp.	bacon fat or vegetable oil	30 mL
1	medium onion, minced	1
1 stalk	celery, thinly sliced	1 stalk
1	small garlic clove, minced	1
1 tbsp.	sweet Hungarian paprika	15 mL
1 cup	beef bouillon (page 148)	250 mL
¼ cup	tomato paste	50 mL
2	red bell peppers, cut in ½'' (1.3 cm) strips	2
2	green bell peppers, cut in ½'' (1.3 cm) strips	2
dash	salt	dash
dash	freshly ground pepper	dash
1 cup	sour cream, for garnish	250 mL
	Noodles Caraway, page 159.	

- Pound beef to a thickness of ½'' (1.3 cm). Sprinkle with flour and salt.
- In a large skillet, heat vegetable oil or bacon fat over medium heat. Add meat in small batches and brown evenly on all sides. Remove from pan and set aside.
- Pour off all but 2 tbsp. (30 mL) fat from skillet. Add onion, celery and sauté over medium heat until soft, about 10 minutes. Stir in garlic and paprika and cook for a few seconds. Add beef bouillon and tomato paste, scraping up any browned bits clinging to bottom of pan. Return beef to skillet and bring to simmer. Cover partially and cook until beef is almost tender — about 40 minutes. If mixture becomes dry, stir in additional stock.
- Add peppers, cover partially and simmer until slightly softened and beef is tender, about 20 minutes. Season to taste with salt and pepper. Spoon over Noodles Caraway and serve with a heaping bowl of sour cream.
- Serves 4.

ALBERTA'S 'BEST' BEEF STICKS

Enjoy spicy, hot-hot beef? Carry on then . . . but do take care to remain reasonably close to fire-fighting equipment!

Combine Beef Sticks with Alberta Baked Beans, page 162, a fresh garden salad and sippets, page 155 — absolutely essential for the removal of even the tiniest morsel of good flavor that might otherwise be left behind!

2 lbs.	*lean sirloin steak cut in ¾" (2 cm) cubes	1 kg
2 tbsp.	crushed chili peppers	30 mL
1	medium onion, quartered	1
2	garlic cloves, minced	2
3 tbsp.	fresh lemon juice	45 mL
2 tbsp.	water	30 mL
1 tbsp.	grated fresh ginger root	15 mL
2 tsp.	salt	10 mL
½ tsp.	freshly ground pepper	2 mL
2 tbsp.	vegetable oil	30 mL
12 approx.	wooden skewers	12 approx.
	Alberta Sauce (below)	

- Combine chili peppers, onion, garlic, lime juice, water, ginger root, salt and pepper in blender; purée until smooth.
- Transfer to large glass bowl. Mix in oil and add beef cubes. Marinate for 2 hours at room temperature or overnight, covered in refrigerator.
- Soak wooden skewers in water for 30 minutes. Thread marinated beef onto skewers; barbecue for about 15-17 minutes or until desired doneness.
- Dip Beef Sticks into Alberta Sauce.
- See photograph opposite.

ALBERTA SAUCE

½ cup	rice vinegar	125 mL
1½ tbsp.	hot prepared mustard	22 mL
2 tbsp.	brown sugar	30 mL
¾ tsp.	soy sauce	3 mL
1 tbsp.	HP sauce	15 mL
2 drops	Tabasco sauce	2 drops
¼ tsp.	salt	1 mL

- Combine all ingredients and let stand for a few hours to let ingredients 'marry'.
- Serves 6.

SOUTH SEAS KABOBS

1 lb.	*lean sirloin tip or round steak in 1½" (3-4 cm) cubes	500 g
19 oz.	can pineapple chunks, drained, pineapple juice reserved	540 mL
1 tbsp.	soy sauce	15 mL
¼ cup	vinegar	50 mL
¼ cup	brown sugar	50 mL
1	green pepper, cut in chunks	1
	onion slivers	
	whole mushrooms	
	cherry tomatoes	

- Marinate beef in mixture of pineapple juice, soy sauce, vinegar and brown sugar for 6-8 hours, covered in refrigerator.
- Remove beef from marinade. Alternate beef and vegetables on skewers. Barbecue approximately 10 minutes or until desired doneness. Brush with sauce and turn kabobs periodically during cooking.
- South Seas kabobs are 'rain proof', great for oven broiling. And you can surprise and delight every member of your family by throwing a tablecloth on the floor, complete with hamper, paper plates, plastic cutlery, napkins and insect repellent. Even teenage sons have been known to participate and have fun. The memory of a rainy day, family den picnic is something that lingers in one's memory book for a long, long time.
- Makes 4 kabobs.

CARPACCIO STEAK

This beef serving isn't for everyone . . . but for those who like 'raw', nothing tastes quite like it. And for those good people who like an adventure every once in awhile . . . try CARPACCIO, see origin page 8.

1 lb.	*lean top sirloin or top round steak partially frozen and sliced paper-thin, against the grain	500 g
¼ cup	olive oil	50 mL
6 dashes	Tabasco sauce	6 dashes
3 tbsp.	chopped shallots	45 mL
2 tbsp.	capers	30 mL
1	lemon, cut into wedges	1
dash	salt	dash
dash	freshly ground pepper	dash
1 tbsp.	finely chopped, fresh parsley	15 mL

- Divide the slices of beef among 6 plates.
- Mix together the olive oil, Tabasco sauce, and shallots and pour equally over beef servings. Marinate 30-60 minutes at room temperature.
- Garnish each plate with capers, a lemon wedge, salt, pepper and parsley.
- Serves 6.

HAMBURGER TARTARE

Make way for the 'hamburger' of hamburgers. Total satisfaction guaranteed with Hamburger Tartare.

2 lbs.	*lean ground sirloin	1 kg
½ cup	chopped onion	125 mL
½	garlic clove, minced	½
½ cup	fresh chopped parsley	125 mL
3 tbsp.	capers, drained	45 mL
⅓ cup	cognac	75 mL
3 tbsp.	Dijon-style mustard	45 mL
2	raw egg yolks	2

- Combine the sirloin, onion, garlic, parsley, capers, cognac, mustard, raw egg yolks, salt and pepper to taste. Shape into 6 patties.
- Broil, fry or grill the hamburgers to desired doneness, or for true aficionados of Steak Tartare, serve raw with buttered pumpernickel or your favorite crackers.
- Serves 6.

STEAK à la PEPPERCORN AND GARLIC

An all-time favorite, a hearty-flavored steak mellowed out with a smidge of butter. A distinct change of pace is needed to finish your meal. BANANAS ROYALE, page 163, served with coffee, feet up, good company, finally turning to a good book. Ahhh, let's leave the dishes 'til morning.

2 x 6 oz.	*lean boneless club steaks	2 x 170 g
1 tbsp.	freshly ground black pepper	15 mL
1 tsp.	dried lemon peel	5 mL
2 tbsp.	lemon juice	30 mL
½ tsp.	Worcestershire sauce	2 mL
dash	Tabasco	dash
1 tbsp.	chopped, fresh parsley	15 mL
2 tsp.	butter	10 mL
2	garlic cloves, minced	2

- Press 1½ tsp. (7 mL) freshly ground pepper into each steak.

- Combine lemon peel, lemon juice, Worcestershire sauce and Tabasco sauce; set aside. In another bowl mix parsley, butter and garlic and form into 2 equal balls. Chill until firm.

- Broil or barbecue to desired doneness. Sprinkle lemon juice mixture over steak while broiling. Serve each steak with a lemon twist and a garlic butter ball.

- Serves 2.

STEAK AND VEGETABLE KABOB

2 lbs.	*lean sirloin beefsteak, cut in 1" (2.5 cm) pieces	1 kg
1 cup	dry sherry	250 mL
¼ cup	vegetable oil	50 mL
3 tbsp.	onion soup mix	45 mL
½ tsp.	dried, crushed, thyme	2 mL
1 tsp.	salt	5 mL
½ tsp.	pepper, freshly ground	2 mL
1	small garlic clove, minced	1
2	zucchini, cut in 1" (2.5 cm) slices	2
	whole fresh mushrooms	
	green or red pepper, cut into ½" (1 cm) slices	
	onion slivers	
	cherry tomatoes	

- Combine sherry, oil, dry onion soup mix, salt, thyme, pepper and garlic in bowl. Add meat; stir to coat. Cover and marinate at room temperature for 2 hours, or overnight in refrigerator.
- Drain meat, reserving marinade. Using skewers, thread meat alternately with zucchini, mushrooms, green peppers and onions.
- Barbecue kabobs 4-6" (10-15 cm) from heat until all sides are browned, allowing 8 minutes total broiling time. Give kabobs a quarter turn every 2 minutes, brushing with a little reserved marinade.
- After removing from barbecue, add a cherry tomato to each skewer.
- Serves 6.
- See photograph, page 48.

SHISH KABOB SPECTACTULAR

*One of the most enjoyable and surprisingly easy ways of entertaining. Simply set out dishes containing chunks of all sorts of foods and appropriate sauces and, of course, *LEAN BEEF and let your guests* **create** *and* **cook** whatever combinations they put on their skewers.

CAUTION, do try and remember which skewers belong to whom, you might even want to consider name tags. The most incredible thing happens, every other kabob looks better than the one you created and cooked, thus causing a goodly amount of discussion and denying as to which belongs to whom!

SATAY

This delicious recipe is a 'must' to remember 365 days of the year. During the balmy summer months, when everyone is 'hamburgered out', Satay is a most welcome treat and, when during our long winter months you would like to recall those wonderful summer evenings, try Satay on the broil along with a rice beer!

1½ lbs.	*lean round beef, inside, outside round steak or a roast	750 g
¼ cup	butter	50 mL
1 tbsp.	lemon juice	15 mL
½ tsp.	Tabasco sauce	2 mL
3 tbsp.	grated onion	45 mL
3 tbsp.	brown sugar	45 mL
1 tsp.	coriander	5 mL
½ tsp.	ground cumin	2 mL
¼ tsp.	ginger	1 mL
1	garlic clove, crushed	1
½ cup	soy sauce	125 mL
dash	salt and pepper	dash
8	wooden skewers	8

- Cut beef into ¾'' (1.5 cm) cubes and place in a shallow dish for marinating.
- Melt butter in a saucepan and add remaining ingredients. Bring to a boil and simmer for 5 minutes. Pour sauce over meat, cover and marinate overnight in refrigerator. Remember to turn the meat from time to time.
- Soak wooden skewers in water for 1 hour prior to use. This prevents them from burning too quickly.
- Remove the meat from marinade and place 5 or 6 pieces on each skewer. Reserve marinade.
- Set oven control to broil. Place skewers on broiling pan and broil 1 side for 7-8 minutes. Turn and brush with reserve marinade and broil for another 7-8 minutes.

OR

- Barbecue for 15 minutes or until done. Brush with reserve marinade and turn frequently.
- Serve Satay with long-grain or wild rice and a vegetable side dish.
- Serves 4.
- See photograph page 48.

GINGER BEEF KABOBS

Cozy the cooked skewered beef up to a bed of wild rice, and for good measure throw in a crisp, green vegetable, a tossed salad with, depending on your fire-fighting skills, a mean or mellow dressing!

2 lbs.	*lean round or flank steak	1 kg
¼ cup	oil	50 mL
¼ cup	firmly packed brown sugar	50 mL
⅓ cup	dry sherry	75 mL
½ cup	soy sauce	125 mL
1	garlic clove, minced	1
1 tsp.	minced fresh ginger root	5 mL
OR		
½ tsp.	dry ginger	2 mL
4	green onions, coarsely chopped	4
	water chestnuts	

- Beef, when slightly frozen or even chilled, is much easier to slice.
- Holding a knife at a 45° angle, diagonally slice beef into strips ⅛" (3 mm) thick.
- Thoroughly mix together oil, brown sugar, sherry, soy sauce, garlic, ginger and chopped green onions. Add beef strips and marinate, covered, for 6 hours or longer, in refrigerator.
- Remove beef from marinade and thread on skewers, slipping a piece of green onion or a water chestnut between each piece of beef. Place skewers over hot coals. Turn occasionally and brush with marinade until tender and nicely browned.
- Serves 4.

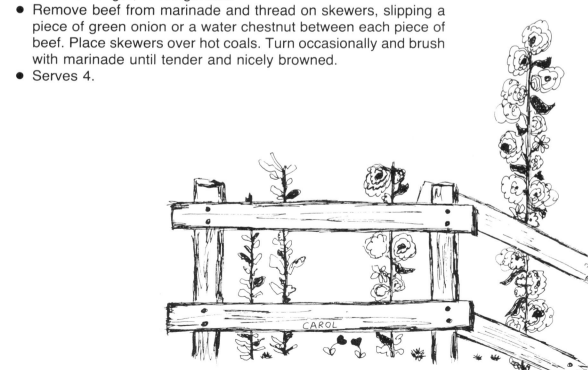

GINGER STEAK WITH GARLIC

Ginger is an exotic spice which has only recently achieved the widespread use and prominence in Western cooking that it has enjoyed for thousands of years in Eastern cuisine.

Add ginger to garlic, combine to serve along with *LEAN flank steak and you have quite a taste treat. Fresh garden vegetables and a Tomato and Basil Salad, page 156, will provide a delicate harmony for the distinctive flavor and aroma of ginger and garlic.

1-2 lbs.	*lean flank steak	0.5-1 kg
1 tbsp.	soy sauce	15 mL
1 tbsp.	sesame oil	15 mL
	Garlic Ginger Sauce, see below	

- Preheat broiler. Sprinkle both sides of the steak with soy sauce and sesame oil and rub into the meat. Broil approximately 6" (15 cm) from heat for 5 to 7 minutes per side, depending on desired doneness. Cut the steak diagonally **across** the grain into thin pieces.
- Overlap 5 or 6 slices on each serving plate and top with several spoonfuls of the garlic ginger sauce. Serve hot or at room temperature.
- Serves 6.

GARLIC GINGER SAUCE

¾ cup	olive oil	175 mL
5	garlic cloves, finely minced	5
3 tbsp.	chopped ginger root, fresh	45 mL
4	carrots, peeled, diced	4
5	scallions (green onions) white part and 2" (5 cm)) green	5
1 cup	dry white wine	250 mL
½ cup	water	125 mL
2 tbsp.	lime juice	30 mL
1 tsp.	turmeric	5 mL
1 tsp.	dried oregano	5 mL
½ tsp.	coriander	2 mL
pinch	red pepper flakes	pinch
½ cup	chopped fresh parsley	125 mL
dash	salt and pepper	dash

- To make sauce, heat oil in skillet over medium heat. Add garlic, ginger and carrots and sauté for 10 minutes. Add scallions and sauté for 2 minutes more. Add wine, water, lime juice, oregano and red pepper flakes. Simmer uncovered over low heat for 30 minutes.
- Stir in the parsley and season to taste with salt and pepper. Makes 3½ cups (875 mL).

BEEF TERIYAKI STEAK

When you hear the word teriyaki it means food which has been marinated in a mixture of soy sauce, fresh ginger root and/or garlic and cooked on a grill or broiled. Teri means 'glossy shine or glaze' and yaki means 'broiled or baked.'

Beef Teriyaki Steak is an absolute palate pleaser. The beef is tender and juicy, the flavor is hearty but not overwhelming and it welcomes almost any other dish you might think of to complete your meal; warm, crusty rolls with butter sliding over the side, cauliflower with a mild cheese sauce, new potatoes with jackets scrubbed clean and cooked whole so as to maintain all that delicious flavor. Here's the place for a repeat of that great Spinach Salad, page 153, you made last week. Say, do you think we could come to your place for dinner?

1 lb.	*lean round steak (inside or outside round)	500 g

TERIYAKI SAUCE

2 tsp.	grated ginger root	10 mL
¼ cup	soy sauce	50 mL
1 tbsp.	white wine	15 mL
½ tsp.	sugar	2 mL
1	garlic clove, crushed	1

● Mix all teriyaki ingredients together. Pour over steaks, cover and refrigerate for 4 hours or overnight. Turn at least once during that time.

*BARBECUE

Teriyaki sauces scorch easily. You must, therefore, adjust temperature and cooking times accordingly. Remember to turn your steaks with tongs rather than using a fork. A fork pierces the meat, allowing the juices to escape. When little bubbles appear on the surface . . . it is time to turn the steak thereby allowing the juices to flow down through the steak again. Don't forget to brush on the reserved teriyaki sauce when you turn the steaks.

*OVEN BROIL

Set oven control to broil — 550°F (290°C). Broil 5-6 minutes each side for medium rare. When turning, remember to brush steak with teriyaki sauce.

MAPLE-MARINATED STEAK

Maple syrup, considered by many Canadians as an important part of their heritage, has enjoyed a phenomenal increase in contemporary applications over the past few years.

It really is hard to surpass the exquisite flavor of beef that has been marinated in maple syrup.

1½-2 lbs.	***lean flank or inside round steak**	.75-1 kg
1 cup	maple syrup	250 mL
2 tbsp.	soy sauce	30 mL
2 tbsp.	lemon juice	30 mL
4 tbsp.	white vinegar	60 mL
2 tbsp.	red wine vinegar	30 mL
1 tsp.	salt	5 mL
½ tsp.	freshly ground pepper	2 mL
1	garlic clove, minced	1

- Thoroughly mix all marinade ingredients. Place steak in large shallow dish and pour marinade over top. Cover and refrigerate for 8 hours or overnight.
- Remove steak. Pour marinade into small saucepan and heat over low heat.
- Barbecue steaks until desired doneness.
- Cutting **across** the grain, cut steak into very thin slices. Place in large serving dish along with heated marinade.
- Serves 4-6.

MANDARIN BEEF STIR-FRY

Succulent beef strips, crisp vegetables, and just enough orange sections to have you looking for seconds are combined in this light and easy beef presentation. Certainly company fare . . . but simple and quick enough to frequently serve and spoil your family!

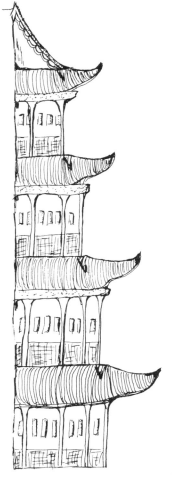

1 lb.	*lean round, steak or roast cut into ½ x 2 in (1 x 5 cm) strips	500 g
½ cup	orange juice	125 mL
1	rind from 1 orange	1
¼ cup	soy sauce	50 mL
¼ tsp.	ginger	1 mL
¼ tsp.	garlic powder	1 mL
2 tbsp.	oil	30 mL
1	onion, medium, sliced	1
2 cups	broccoli florets	500 mL
2 tbsp.	water	30 mL
1 cup	mushrooms, fresh	250 mL
1	green pepper, medium, sliced	1
10 oz.	mandarin oranges	284 mL
2 tbsp.	cornstarch	30 mL

- Tenderize beef with mallet.
- Marinate meat in a combination of orange juice, orange rind, soy sauce, ginger and garlic powder, covered, overnight in refrigerator.
- Prepare vegetables. Heat oil in wok or frying pan. Add onions, broccoli, and water. Stir well. Add mushrooms and green pepper. Cook uncovered for one minute and then move vegetables to the side of wok.
- Drain beef, reserving marinade. Stir-fry beef until color changes, then mix with vegetables. Add orange segments but do not stir.
- Combine reserved marinade with cornstarch then add to wok. Stir gently until sauce thickens.
- Serve immediately over a bed of rice along with fresh, slender green beans. Sprinkle stir-fry with sesame seeds.
- Serves 4 with only 275 calories per serving.

FLANK STEAK à la PÊCHE

PEACHES . . . WITH BEEF . . . PERFECTLY OUTRAGEOUS! Ssshh . . . but do you think that I could try them?

2	*lean flank steaks, 1¼ lbs. (625 g) each	2

MEAT MARINADE

¾ cup	ketchup	175 mL
¼ cup	Worcestershire sauce	50 mL
3 tbsp.	HP sauce	45 mL
¼ cup	lemon juice	50 mL
½ cup	port wine	125 mL
¼ cup	vegetable oil	50 mL
2	garlic cloves, minced	2
1 tbsp.	Dijon-style mustard	15 mL
½ tsp.	salt	2 mL
¼ tsp.	pepper	1 mL
½ tsp.	crushed chili peppers	2 mL

PEACH MARINADE

¾ cup	port wine	175 mL
1 tbsp.	lemon juice	15 mL
28 oz.	can peach halves, drained, syrup reserved	796 mL

GARNISH — Fresh parsley

- On each side of steak make shallow diagonal cuts in a diamond pattern. Place in large casserole dish.
- Combine ketchup, Worcestershire, HP sauce, ½ cup (125 mL) reserved peach syrup, lemon juice, port, oil, garlic, mustard, salt, pepper and crushed chili peppers. Pour over steaks, cover and refrigerate, turning occasionally for several hours or overnight.
- For peach marinade combine port and lemon juice. Drain peaches. Add peach halves to marinade, cover and refrigerate for at least 2 hours.
- Drain steaks, reserving meat marinade. Broil, brushing occasionally with marinade, for 5-7 minutes on each side or until desired doneness.
- In saucepan, thoroughly mix peach marinade and remaining meat marinade. Bring to boil, reduce heat and keep warm.
- Serving — slice steaks thinly **across** grain in diagonal slices and place on serving platter. Remove peach halves from marinade mixture with slotted spoon and place around steak, garnish with parsley. Pass warm marinade.
- Serves 6-8.
- See photograph, page 64.

SZECHWAN SHREDDED BEEF

You needn't attend an expensive Chinese restaurant to enjoy one of to-day's most popular menu items. Beef, vegetables and noodles . . . all-in-one cooking and serving. Have fun around the family table and also serve Chinese tea and fortune cookies after this delicious rendering of beef.

Hoisin sauce will, if transferred to a glass jar and refrigerated, last for many months.

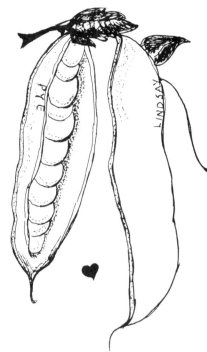

¾-1 lb.	*lean beef flank steak	350-500 g
1 tbsp.	dry sherry	15 mL
1 tbsp.	soy sauce	15 mL
2 tbsp.	hoisin sauce	30 mL
1 tbsp.	cornstarch	15 mL
½ cup	vegetable oil	125 mL
½ cup	shredded bamboo shoots	125 mL
½ cup	shredded carrots	125 mL
½ cup	shredded snow peas	125 mL
1 tsp.	salt	5 mL
dash	freshly ground pepper	dash
2 tsp.	shredded fresh ginger root	10 mL
½ tsp.	chili pepper flakes	2 mL

- Thoroughly chill, or better still, lightly freeze flank steak. This will make slicing into very thin slices much easier.
- Slice the beef **against** the grain into very thin slices, then shred the slices. Combine the beef shreds, sherry, soy sauce, hoisin sauce and cornstarch.
- Heat 2 tbsp. (30 mL) oil in skillet or wok and stir fry the bamboo shoots, carrots and snow peas for 1 minute. Add salt, pepper, stir and remove the vegetables from the skillet and set aside.
- In the same skillet or wok, heat 6 tbsp. (90 mL) of oil. Stir in ginger. Add the beef mixture and stir fry for 2 minutes. Add the chili pepper flakes and mix well. Drain off any excess oil.
- Return the cooked vegetables to the wok for 1 minute, mixing thoroughly.
- Arrange Szechwan Shredded Beef over steamed white rice and serve hot.
- Serves 4.

TERIYAKI BEEF STRIPS

FANTASTIC . . . probably the best word to describe Teriyaki Beef Strips. Marinated 'melt-in-your-mouth' beef cooked to perfection and surrounded by delightfully crisp and delicate snow peas.

What a perfect time to serve your best version of Spinach Salad, page 153. The traditional sweet and sour dressing of a Spinach Salad offers a nice balance to the beef strips. Don't forget the sesame bread sticks!

1 lb.	*lean round or blade steak or roast	500 g
½ cup	Teriyaki sauce/marinade	125 mL
¾ cup	orange juice	175 mL
2 tbsp.	vegetable oil	30 mL
1	medium onion sliced	1
1 cup	sliced, fresh mushrooms	250 mL
¾ cup	snow peas, fresh or frozen	175 mL
1	medium green pepper sliced	1
10 oz.	can mandarin oranges, drained	284 mL
2 tbsp.	cornstarch	30 mL

TERIYAKI MARINADE

2 tsp.	grated ginger root	10 mL
¼ cup	soy sauce	50 mL
1 tbsp.	white wine	15 mL
½ tsp.	sugar	2 mL
1	garlic clove, minced	1
	finely grated orange rind	

- Cut meat across the grain into thin strips. Combine all ingredients in Teriyaki marinade and ½ cup (125 mL) orange juice. Add beef strips, cover and refrigerate 8-10 hours or overnight.
- Remove beef strips from marinade. Pat dry. Reserve marinade.
- In wok or frying pan, heat oil. Add vegetables and stir well. Add ¼ cup (50 mL) orange juice. Cover and cook over medium heat for 2 minutes.
- Add beef to vegetable mixture and cook 1 minute. Add orange segments, cover and cook 1 minute.
- Quickly combine reserved marinade with cornstarch, add to pan. Stir gently, cover, cook for 1 minute. Do not OVERCOOK beef.
- Serves 5.

CHINESE SWEET AND SOUR BEEF

This beef dish is worth every minute of the precision work needed to bring it to the table with texture and flavor at the peak of perfection.

Chinese tea, chop sticks, steamed white rice and, last but not least, fortune cookies, provide the perfect ambience for the family mahjong championship!

1¼ lb.	*lean inside, outside round beef, trimmed and cut in ¾" (2 cm) thick cubes	600 g
1	egg	1
6 tbsp.	cornstarch	90 mL
1½ tbsp.	all-purpose flour	22 mL
dash	pepper, freshly ground	dash
¼ cup	soy sauce	50 mL
3 tbsp.	dry sherry	45 mL
1 cup	cold beef bouillon (see page 148)	250 mL
	vegetable oil	
1 tbsp.	peanut oil	15 mL
1	garlic clove, minced	1
	salt	
3 tbsp.	ketchup	45 mL
⅓ cup	red wine vinegar	75 mL
1	orange, juice of	1
1½ tsp.	lemon juice, fresh	7 mL
⅓ cup	sugar	75 mL
1	small red bell pepper, cut into strips	1
2	carrots, cut into thin sticks	2
2 stalks	celery, cut into ½" (1.5 cm)	2 stalks
	celery leaves, chopped coarsely	
2 tbsp.	cold water	30 mL

- Separate egg, refrigerate white. Set aside 1 heaping tbsp. (20 mL) cornstarch.
- Whisk egg yolk with remaining cornstarch, flour and pepper. Blend in 1 tbsp. (15 mL) each soy sauce and sherry. Add enough beef bouillon to make a smooth batter that is thick enough to coat meat cubes. Cover and let stand 30 minutes.
- Combine 2 tbsp. (30 mL) each soy sauce and sherry. Add meat cubes, cover and marinate 10 minutes, stirring several times.
- Preheat oven to 275°F (140°C). Line baking sheet with paper towels and place in oven.
- Beat egg white until stiff and fold into prepared batter. Coat meat cubes with batter and quickly fry in a deep skillet until golden brown. Remove with slotted spoon, placing on cooking tray covered with paper towels. Keep warm.

- Heat peanut oil in skillet. Add garlic and cook over medium heat until translucent. Season with salt. Add remaining soy sauce, ketchup, vinegar, orange and lemon juices and sugar. Cook, stirring until sugar is dissolved.
- Pour in remaining meat bouillon and bring to a boil. Add vegetables, except celery leaves, and cook over medium-low heat until tender and crisp, about 6-8 minutes.
- Mix remaining cornstarch with water and stir in vegetables. Bring to boil. If necessary, adjust seasoning.
- Stir in meat cubes and sprinkle with celery leaves. Serve immediately with steamed rice.
- Serves 4.

MOCK DUCK

An unusual treat! Even game enthusiasts will enjoy this flank steak and stuffing dish, complemented by a cranberry sauce . . . especially during one of those frequent December evenings when snowflakes and winter winds dance and swirl about.

2 lbs.	*lean flank steak	1 kg
1 tbsp.	salt	15 mL
1 cup	bread crumbs	250 mL
¼ cup	chopped onions	50 mL
1 tsp.	poultry seasoning	5 mL
dash	freshly ground pepper	dash
½ cup	raw, chopped carrot OR	125 mL
½ cup	chopped celery	125 mL
¼ cup	bacon fat	50 mL
1 cup	water	250 mL

- Preheat oven to 350°F (180°C).
- Sprinkle salt over the flank steak.
- In a bowl combine bread crumbs, onion, poultry seasoning, pepper and carrot OR celery. Mix thoroughly.
- Spread mixture over the surface of the flank steak. Roll steak up as in a 'jelly roll' and tie securely in several places.
- In a heavy skillet heat bacon fat. Sauté mock duck until brown on all sides. Place mock duck in large casserole dish.
- Add water, cover and bake at 350°F (180°C) for 2 hours.
- Whole cranberry sauce slightly warmed is an absolute must!
- Serves 4.

ROULADEN

This recipe will serve 4 . . . however, if you're really quiet and no one except your 'other half' knows that Rouladen is in the making . . . there will be more for you to enjoy. And you will enjoy!

A delectable filling, juicy beef, topped off with a gentle sauce. Parsley potatoes, a green vegetable, tossed salad and bread sticks . . . maybe you should share this treat. You'll enjoy the rave reviews.

4 x 5 oz.	roulades *lean beef, inside outside, round	4 x 140 g
3-4 oz.	bacon, cut into thin strips	85-115 g
2	dill pickles, cut in thin strips & patted dry	2
1 tbsp.	mustard	15 mL
dash	salt	dash
dash	freshly ground pepper	dash
1	onion, thinly sliced	1
2 tbsp.	vegetable oil	30 mL
1½ cups	beef bouillon (page 148)	375 mL
1 cup	sour cream (optional)	250 mL

- After patting meat dry with paper towels, flatten (tenderize) meat with palm of hand. Do not use a mallet as this will crush the delicate fibers.
- Cover meat with a thin layer of mustard, salt and pepper. Distribute bacon, onion and pickle evenly over the meat.
- Starting at narrow end, roll up meat, tucking in the ends to enclose filling completely. Secure each roll with a skewer. Season with salt and pepper.
- In a skillet large enough to hold all roulades, add oil and place over heat until very hot. Brown rolls evenly on all sides. If meat is cooked until brown and crusty, juices will not escape during braising and meat will remain tender and moist.
- Add bouillon to skillet and scrape up those flavorful browned bits from the bottom. Cover and cook over low heat simmering gently for about 1½ hours. Do not let liquid boil as this will toughen meat.
- Remove Rouladen from skillet, keep warm. Bring braising liquid to a boil and whisk in sour cream. Cook sauce uncovered over medium heat, stirring constantly until reduced to desired consistency.
- Voila! Pour sauce over Rouladen and enjoy.
- Serves 4.

BEEF JERKY

There are thousands of good reasons to have an ample supply of Beef Jerky available, not the least of which is 'simple enjoyment.'

2 lbs.	*lean flank steak	1 kg
¼ cup	soy sauce	50 mL
1 cup	ketchup	250 mL
¼ cup	Worcestershire sauce	50 mL
2 tbsp.	HP sauce	30 mL
4 drops	Tabasco sauce	4 drops
½ tsp.	salt	2 mL
¼ tsp.	freshly ground pepper	1 mL
2	small garlic cloves, minced	2
1 tbsp.	finely chopped onion	15 mL
¼ cup	red wine vinegar	50 mL
2 tbsp.	vegetable oil	30 mL

- If the flank steak is partially frozen it will be easier to slice, along the grain, into ⅛" (3 mm) thick strips.
- Combine all other ingredients and mix thoroughly. Add beef strips, cover and marinate in refrigerator for 8-12 hours or overnight. Stir occasionally, making sure all sides of strips are coated.
- Prepare oven racks by **lightly** moistening with vegetable oil. Lay beef strips on racks, making sure they do not overlap.
- Cook at 150°F (70°C) for 8-10 hours. For most ovens this temperature reading is a 'warming' setting. It is therefore difficult to say exactly how long to cook jerky. RULE OF THUMB — when strips are slightly stiff and have only the barest hint of color left on the inside, they are done.
- Let jerky sit on the cupboard for an hour or so, then place in an airtight jar or container.
- Makes approximately 60 strips . . . which around our home lasts 2, maybe 3 days. Perhaps you don't have as many 'grumblies' as we do!

MATAMBRE

In Europe, this spicy beef roll would be called a roulade. However, this recipe dates circa 1900 — when travellers crossing Argentina in stagecoaches carried a roll of beef to see them through the journey. Matambre, from 'mata hambre', literally means, 'it kills hunger'.

Aside from the provocative taste of Matambre — its presentation is colorful and mouth-watering. Wrapped inside the flank steak, jelly-roll fashion, are green peppers, chopped pimiento, corn, chili peppers, carrots and peas.

Hot or cold — enjoy this peppy, vegetable-studded beef dish!

2 x 2 lb.	*lean flank steaks	2 x 1 kg
1 cup	frozen, mixed vegetables	250 mL
½ cup	finely chopped onion	125 mL
¼ cup	finely chopped green pepper	50 mL
¼ cup	chopped celery	50 mL
¼ cup	finely minced pimiento	50 mL
2 tsp.	finely minced chili pepper	10 mL
1	garlic clove, crushed	1
1 tsp.	salt	5 mL
½ tsp.	freshly ground pepper	2 mL
2	hard-cooked eggs, quartered	2
1 cup	beef bouillon (page 148)	250 mL
1 stalk	celery, sliced	1 stalk
1	carrot, sliced	1
1	onion, sliced	1
1	garlic clove, chopped	1
	chili sauce	

- Ask your butcher to butterfly the steaks. However, it is surely something that you can do yourself. Starting at 1 side (not end) cut through the steak **almost** to the other side. Be careful that you don't cut all the way through or you will end up with 2 separate pieces. Open the steak and pound it flat. Remove any excess fat and cut the edges straight so that the finished steaks are roughly square — about 12" x 12" (30 x 30 cm).
- Preheat oven to 350°F (180°C).
- Lay the steaks side by side, overlapping the edges 1-2" (2.5-5 cm), so that when you roll them they hold together as if they were 1 piece of meat. Combine the mixed vegetables, onion, celery, green pepper, pimiento, chili pepper, crushed garlic, salt and pepper; mix thoroughly.
- Spread this mixture evenly over the steaks, covering the entire surface. Evenly distribute quartered eggs across the meat. Rollup the 2 steaks jelly-roll style, as tightly as possible. Secure the beef roll with string tied about every 2" (5 cm).

- Place the Matambre in a shallow casserole and add the beef bouillon, sliced celery, carrot, onions and chopped garlic. Cover and braise for 2 hours, basting the meat frequently.
- Move the Matambre to a platter for about 10 minutes before serving. This makes the meat a little firmer and thus carving is easier. Cut the Matambre roll in 1'' (2.5 cm) slices and serve with chili sauce.
- Serves 6.

CHILI SAUCE

4 tbsp.	butter	60 mL
1	onion, finely chopped	1
1	green pepper, finely chopped	1
1 stalk	celery	1 stalk
1	garlic clove, minced	1
2 tbsp.	flour	30 mL
1½ tbsp.	chili powder	22 mL
1 tsp.	salt	5 mL
¼ tsp.	freshly ground pepper	1 mL
1 cup	tomato juice	250 mL
1 cup	beef bouillon (page 148)	250 mL

- Melt butter in large skillet. Sauté onion, green pepper, celery and garlic in melted butter until vegetables are translucent but not browned, or about 5 minutes.
- Blend in the flour, chili powder, salt and pepper. Stir over low heat for 2 minutes. Stir in the tomato juice and beef bouillon. Cook, stirring over medium heat until slightly thickened. Serve hot.

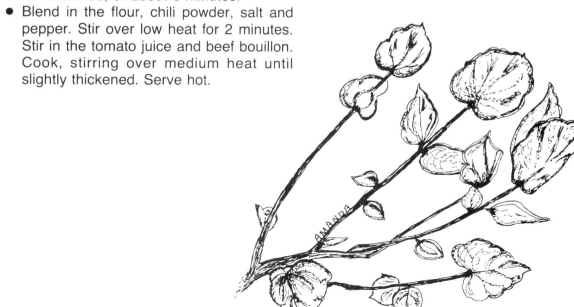

COGNAC BEEF ROULADES

Elegant fare, simple to make and spectacular to set on the table 'flaming.' There won't be an eye that isn't saucer-wide in anticipation of this beef dish.

1½ lbs. or more	*lean beef rouladen (or inside, outside round, pounded almost paper thin)	750 g
4 oz.	mushroom pieces	125 g
1 tbsp.	chopped onions	15 mL
½ cup	crumbled Roquefort cheese, packed	125 mL
1 tsp.	salt	5 mL
¼ tsp.	pepper	1 mL
2 tbsp.	flour	30 mL
2 tbsp.	butter	30 mL
1¼ cup	tomato vegetable juice	300 mL
¼ cup	Hennessey Cognac	50 mL
1 tbsp.	Worcestershire sauce	15 mL

- Drain mushroom pieces, reserving juices. Combine mushrooms, onion, ¼ cup (50 mL) crumbled Roquefort, salt and pepper. Sprinkle mixture over steaks. Roll up steaks jelly-roll fashion and fasten securely with skewers. Roll in flour.
- In large skillet, heat butter and brown roulades evenly on all sides. Combine juice drained from mushrooms, tomato vegetable juice, cognac and Worcestershire.
- Pour mixture over beef. Cover tightly. Simmer 40 minutes or until tender. Sprinkle remaining ¼ cup (50 mL) of Roquefort over each steak.
- Be spectacular and daring, serve **flaming** beef roulades. Just before serving, carefully light the cognac!!
- Sometimes the cover over the beef is not airtight, thus allowing evaporation of the cognac. If you are unable to establish a flame over roulades, simply add a touch more cognac to the dish and then relight.
- For a wine with enough character to provide compatability with roulades try a Cabernet Sauvignon.
- Serves 4-6.

MILWAUKEE BEER 'N' BEEF

3 lbs.	*lean round, blade or cross rib steak	1.5 kg
12 oz.	beer	341 mL
¼ cup	oil	50 mL
2 tbsp.	cider vinegar	30 mL
2 tbsp.	brown sugar	30 mL
3	onions, thinly sliced	3
2	garlic cloves, minced	2
1	bay leaf	1
½ tsp.	thyme	2 mL
½ tsp.	salt	2 mL
¼ tsp.	freshly ground pepper	1 mL
4 slices	bacon, cut into 4 pieces each	4 slices
	chopped fresh parsley	

- Combine beer, oil, vinegar, sugar, 1 sliced onion, garlic, bay leaf, thyme, salt, pepper and mix well. Pierce steak several times with a skewer. Place steak in a bowl and pour marinade over it. Cover and refrigerate 8 hours or overnight.
- Reserve marinade after removing beef. Broil steaks to desired doneness. Great on the barbecue too! Brush occasionally with marinade.
- In a skillet cook bacon, set aside. Place remaining sliced onions in skillet and cook until well browned, add a pinch of brown sugar and season to taste.
- To serve, slice steak across the grain in thin slices and cover each serving with onions and bacon pieces. A small amount of reheated marinade may be used as a sauce when serving.
- A tossed green salad with a delicate oil and vinegar dressing . . . warm, crispy, crunchy rolls . . . firm, cold, freshly sliced tomatoes served along with Milwaukee Beef 'n' Beer will provide a hearty meal for 6.
- DESSERT . . . a 'cinnamony and brown sugar' BAKED APPLE page 163, with just a dollop of ice cream.
- Serves 6.

CONTINENTAL STEAK . . . BARBECUED

A steaming baked potato, fresh, slender, green beans, sliced and seasoned cucumbers triumphantly set the stage for a steak deliciously cooked to perfection and then topped with orange butter. Who could possibly ask for more? I know, I know, just 'more' often!

2 lbs.	*lean blade, cross rib or outside (bottom) round steak	1 kg
½ cup	soy sauce	125 mL
⅓ cup	horseradish	75 mL
¼ cup	red wine vinegar	50 mL
¼ cup	lemon juice	50 mL
3 tbsp.	lime juice	45 mL
2 tbsp.	oil	30 mL
2 tbsp.	Worcestershire sauce	30 mL
1 tbsp.	parsley	15 mL
2 tbsp.	dry mustard	30 mL
2	garlic cloves, minced	2

- Combine all ingredients except meat. Mix well and pour over steak. Cover and refrigerate overnight.
- Drain meat, reserving marinade. Barbecue steak 5-6 minutes for rare or to desired doneness. Brush with marinade during cooking. If desired, heat marinade and serve with steak.
- Serves 8.

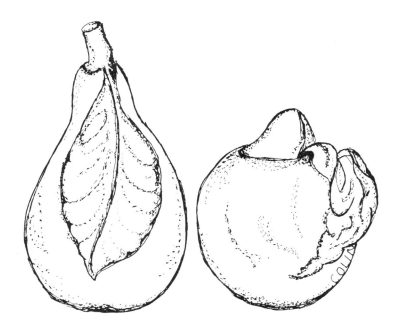

GROUND BEEF

- BUYING GUIDE

- MEAT LOAVES

- MEATBALLS

- CASSEROLES AND STUFFED VEGETABLES

- PASTA PARTNERS

- CRÊPES AND BREADS

- MEAT PIES AND TURNOVERS

WHAT IS THE DIFFERENCE BETWEEN LEAN, MEDIUM AND REGULAR GROUND BEEF?

	LEAN	MEDIUM	REGULAR
Fat Content	No more than 17%	No more than 23%	No more than 30%
Cooking Suggestions	Recipes in which the beef is not precooked before adding to other ingredients and for low-calorie recipes.	Recipes in which the ground beef is not precooked before adding to other ingredients.	Recipes in which the meat is cooked and fat is drained before being added to other ingredients in the recipe.
Examples	Cabbage Rolls Meat Loaf	Meat Balls Salisbury Steak	Meat Patties Spaghetti Sauce Tacos
Price Range	Higher	Medium	Lower
Advantages	Low in calories. Produces firm product.	Holds shape well. Produces firm product.	Economical. Moist and juicy product.

yummy garlic

Comparing costs? . . . Use this formula:

Medium ground beef is a good buy compared to regular, if the cost is less than 10% over the price of regular ground beef.

Lean ground beef is a good buy compared to regular if the cost is less than 20% over the price of regular.

It is natural for the inside of a package of ground beef to be a dark red while the outside is bright red. This color difference is due to oxidation. Oxygen has brightened the beef on the outside, but it could not reach the beef on the inside.

SICILIAN MEAT ROLL

We make you an offer you cannot refuse, MAKE THIS DELICIOUS RECIPE or else you'll be sorry, because it really is delicious. Delicious enough in fact, to invite the whole family. But tell them, their end is to bring a bottle of Chianti. Wine, beef, vegetables, salad, fresh hot bread, cool Sicilian Spumoni ice cream for dessert, and a 'great catch up' of family gossip, what a time, what a time!

2 lbs.	*lean ground beef	1 kg
2	eggs, beaten	2
½ cup	tomato sauce	125 mL
¾ cup	soft bread crumbs	175 mL
2 tbsp.	snipped parsley	30 mL
½ tsp.	dried, crushed oregano	2 mL
½ tsp.	Italian seasoning	2 mL
¼ tsp.	salt	1 mL
dash	pepper	dash
1	garlic clove, crushed	1
4-6 oz.	cooked ham, thinly sliced	125-170 g
½ cup	grated mozzarella cheese	125 mL
	sliced mozzarella cheese	

- Combine eggs and tomato sauce in a large bowl. Stir in bread crumbs, parsley, oregano, Italian seasoning, salt, pepper and garlic. Add ground beef and mix well.
- Place a 12" x 10" (30 cm x 25 cm) sheet of foil on a flat surface. Place the meat mixture on foil and carefully pat meat into a 10" x 8" x 1" (25 x 20 x 2.5 cm) rectangle.
- Arrange ham slices on top of meat, leaving a small margin around the edges. Sprinkle grated cheese evenly on top of the ham.
- Beginning at the short end, carefully roll up meat, using foil to lift; seal edges and ends. Place roll, seam side down, in a 13" x 9" x 2" (33 x 23 x 5 cm) pan.
- Bake at 350°F (180°C) for approximately 1¼ hours. Remember the center will remain pink due to the ham. Remove any excess fat.
- Add cheese slices to top of roll and return to oven for 2 minutes or until cheese melts. Remove from oven, place on platter and garnish with parsley.
- Serves 8.

MICRO — MEAT LOAF CLASSIC

So universally accepted is the Classic Meat Loaf that it had to become part of our repertoire.

No. 2, Opus 46 Appassionato should include a French Salad Bowl with Bacon and Spinach, page 153, well-seasoned vegetables and cheese bread.

2 lbs.	*lean ground beef	1 kg
7½ oz.	can tomato sauce, divided	213 mL
¼ cup	brown sugar	50 mL
1 tsp.	prepared mustard	5 mL
2	eggs, lightly beaten	2
2 drops	Tabasco sauce	2 drops
1	medium onion minced	1
¼ cup	cracker crumbs	50 mL
1½ tsp.	salt	7 mL
¼ tsp.	freshly ground pepper	1 mL
¼ tsp.	Italian allspice	1 mL

- Combine ½ tomato sauce, brown sugar, and mustard in small bowl. Set aside.
- In large mixing bowl combine eggs, Tabasco sauce, onion, cracker crumbs, ground beef, salt, pepper and Italian allspice. Add ½ cup (125 mL) of tomato sauce mixture and stir thoroughly.
- Place meat mixture in glass ring mold. Pour remaining tomato sauce over top of meat. Cook, uncovered on 100% POWER (High) for 12-14 minutes. Let stand, covered for 5-10 minutes before serving.
- Serves 6.

bay leaves

MEAT LOAF UNDER ORANGE GLAZE

What a treat to encounter, great taste and the convenience of microwave cooking. This recipe offers both and more when served with Tomato and Basil Salad, page 156, and a vegetable side dish.

A quick dessert . . . Bananas Royale, page 163.

1½ lbs.	*lean ground beef	750 g
2	eggs, beaten	2
¾ cup	milk	175 mL
½ cup	fine, dry bread crumbs	125 mL
¼ cup	finely chopped onion	50 mL
2 tbsp.	snipped parsley	30 mL
½ tsp.	ground sage	2 mL
1 tsp.	salt	5 mL
dash	freshly ground pepper	dash
3 tbsp.	light corn syrup	45 mL
2 tsp.	finely shredded orange peel	10 mL
¼ tsp.	dried orange bits	2 mL

- Thoroughly mix eggs and milk. Stir in bread crumbs, onion, parsley, sage, salt and pepper.
- Add meat and mix well. Pat into a 6 cup (1.5 L) ring mold. Carefully unmold into a 9" x 2" (22 x 5 cm) pie plate.
- Cover loosely with waxed paper. Cook in microwave on 100% POWER (High) for 10-12 minutes or until nearly done, rotating a quarter-turn every 3 minutes. Remove excess fat from bottom of pan.
- Combine syrup, orange peel and orange bits. Spoon over meat. Cover with waxed paper. Cook on 100% POWER (High) for 2-3 minutes or until heated through. Let stand, covered, for 5 minutes.
- Serves 6.

COLD MEAT LOAF

Company coming? Twisted lemon slices, snuggled into fresh sprigs of parsley, wrapped around cold meat loaf is an all-time favorite for many party planners. Thinly sliced cold meat loaf, dipped into one of several sauces and placed atop a crunchy cracker, will keep many a guest happy and, in some cases, gratefully quiet!

Has the weatherman promised a summer scorcher? The availability of a cold meat loaf to accompany a crisp green salad and a French baguette will leave you with nothing more pressing than to find a shady spot in which to settle down and enjoy that new book.

I lb.	*lean ground beef	500 g
2 lbs.	sausage meat	1 kg
1 cup	chopped onion	250 mL
4 cups	fine, fresh bread crumbs	1 L
¾ tsp.	poultry seasoning	3 mL
¼ tsp.	celery salt	1 mL
1	egg, lightly beaten	1

- Combine all ingredients in a large bowl and mix thoroughly. Pack meat mixture into a standard loaf pan and bake at 350°F (180°C) for 1¾-2 hours.
- Several times during cooking and when meat loaf is finished remove any accumulated fat with a cooking syringe.
- After about 1 hour cooking time, check to determine if meat loaf is as brown as you would like. If so, loosely cover with foil for the remainder of cooking time.
- When cooked, carefully turn out of pan. Allow meat loaf to cool thoroughly before wrapping and placing in refrigerator.
- Servings will vary with use; buffet 6-8, sandwiches 3-4.

SLOPPY JOES

Great fare for the young crowd! Sloppy Joes, cool punch and a gooey dessert will earn 'brownie points.' Much needed brownie points that can be exchanged the next time the lawn needs cutting or the dishes washed. Probably the most rugged endeavour on a day to day basis for most parents is 'staying ahead' of those fast-thinking, even faster-talking teenagers.

However, one must remember that somewhere in the dimly lit past was that overwhelming need to converse with our offspring. Can you remember the times when Dad's homecoming seemed never to arrive, so excited were we with a new word that the little one had just mumbled. And the encouragement we offered . . . 'Tracy, can you say Mooommmee?' All that . . . for the word best remembered, 'WHY?'

1¼ lb.	*lean ground beef	625 g
2 tbsp.	minced onion flakes	30 mL
1 tbsp.	brown sugar	15 mL
2 tbsp.	prepared mustard	30 mL
¾ tsp.	salt	3 mL
1 tbsp.	Worcestershire sauce	15 mL
½ cup	ketchup	125 mL
½ cup	water	125 mL
4	hamburger buns, halved	4

- Slowly brown beef in a large skillet, stirring constantly. Add all remaining ingredients, except buns, and let simmer for 20 minutes.
- Arrange 8 hamburger bun halves on a large shallow baking pan. Spoon Sloppy Joe mixture on top of buns. If desired, sprinkle with grated or sliced Cheddar.
- Bake at 350°F (180°C) for about 25 minutes, until bubbly. Serve immediately.
- Serves 4.

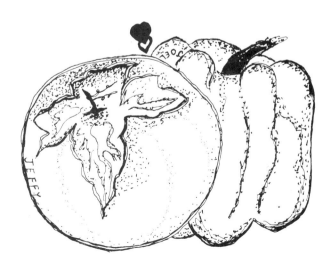

SOUR CREAM STUFFED MEAT LOAF

Proof positive that a feast does not have to be expensive. A slice from this meat loaf fills the air with a subtle savory aroma. What a pleasant sight to behold, each bell pepper filled and surrounded with a delicious meat mixture, colorful and scrumptious.

1¼ lbs.	*lean ground beef	650 g
1½	stale dinner rolls	1½
1½ cups	warm water	375 mL
2	small onions, finely chopped	2
1-2	garlic cloves, finely chopped	1-2
2	dill pickles, finely chopped	2
2 tbsp.	corn relish	30 mL
1-2 tbsp.	capers, drained	15-30 mL
2	eggs	2
½	lemon, juice of	½
dash	salt	dash
dash	pepper	dash
dash	cayenne pepper	dash
2 small	elongated red bell peppers	2 small
1	bunch chives	1
2	bunch herbs (basil, dill and parsley)	2
3 tbsp.	butter	45 mL
½ cup	hot beef bouillon (page 148)	125 mL
¼ cup	heavy (whipping) cream	50 mL
½ cup	sour cream	125 mL
dash	paprika	dash

- Soak dinner roll in warm water until softened. Squeeze roll dry and combine with onion, garlic, pickle, relish, capers, eggs, lemon juice and meat. Mix thoroughly. Season with salt, pepper and cayenne. Place in refrigerator for ½ hour to firm up, making meat mixture easier to handle.
- Cut top and bottom off peppers. Core and seed the peppers.
- Finely chop both top and bottom of peppers and mix into ¾ of meat mixture.
- Finely chop herbs. Mix into remaining ¼ meat mixture. Stuff peppers with this mixture.
- Place oven rack in second position from bottom of oven and preheat oven to 350°F (180°C). Line large loaf pan with enough foil hanging over the edge to assist in the removal of stuffed meat loaf when cooked. Drizzle a small amount of oil on top of foil.
- Place stuffed peppers end to end and form a larger portion of meat mixture into loaf around peppers. Transfer loaf to foil-lined pan and bake 50 minutes, frequently brushing with butter.

SOUR CREAM STUFFED MEAT LOAF (CONT'D.)

- Whisk together meat bouillon, cream, sour cream and paprika. Pour over meat loaf and bake 20 minutes more.
- Transfer loaf to serving platter and surround with sauce. Serve immediately. Additional sour cream as a garnish is very popular in our home.
- Serves 4.

CARAMBA MEAT LOAF

Meat loaf is a favorite beef presentation the world over. We offer a rather unique version that has just a 'touch of dash'. Oven-warmed, crusty, whole-wheat rolls with butter just slipping over the side, baby carrots sprinkled with chopped fresh parsley, and glazed brussels sprouts, will make your dinner companions stand and shout, 'OLE, OLE'!

1½ lbs.	*lean ground beef	700 g
2	eggs, slightly beaten	2
1 cup	soft bread crumbs	250 mL
5 tbsp.	ketchup	75 mL
1	garlic clove, minced	1
2 tbsp.	green chili peppers, rinsed, seeded and chopped	30 mL
¼ tsp.	salt	1 mL
¼ tsp.	chili powder	1 mL
dash	pepper	dash
4 tbsp.	ketchup	60 mL
2 oz.	Monterey Jack cheese, quartered diagonally	4 slices

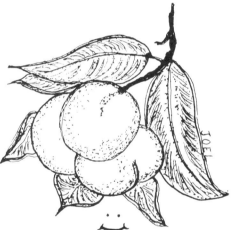

- Combine the egg, bread crumbs, 5 tbsp. (75 mL) ketchup, chopped green chili peppers, garlic, salt, chili powder and pepper. Add ground beef and mix well. Shape meat mixture in a 9" x 5" x 3" (23 x 12 x 7 cm) loaf pan.
- Bake at 350°F (180°C) for 40 minutes. Remove any excess fat.
- Spread remaining 4 tbsp. (60 mL) of ketchup over top of meat loaf. Arrange the cheese slices on top. Return to oven and bake for 5 more minutes or until cheese is melted.
- Serves 4-6.

*MICROWAVE INSTRUCTIONS
- Make meat loaf as directed above. Place loaf in a non-metal 9" x 2" (2.5 L) pie plate.
- Cover with wax paper, cook on 100% POWER (High) for 10-12 minutes or until meat is done. Turn the dish once during cooking. Remove excess fat.
- Spread ketchup and cheese as instructed above. Micro-cook the meat, un-covered for 45 seconds or until cheese is melted.

BRUSSELS SPROUTS GLAZE . . . warm a mixture of ⅓ cup (75 mL) red wine vinegar, a dollop of butter and sugar to slightly sweeten. Pour over sprouts.

BURGUNDY MEATBALLS

Forewarned, they say, is forearmed! Beware, to serve Burgundy meatballs just once is to have to serve Burgundy meatballs forever and ever. Nothing else tastes quite like them!

You will have to become a marketing expert in order to change your family preference and attitude toward trying any other meatball recipe.

¾ lb.	*lean ground beef	340 g
¾ cup	dry bread crumbs	175 mL
1	small onion minced	1
¾ tsp.	cornstarch	3 mL
dash	allspice	dash
1	egg, slightly beaten	1
¾ cup	light cream	175 mL
dash	salt	dash
¼ cup	vegetable oil	50 mL
3 tbsp.	flour	45 mL
2 cups	water	500 mL
1 cup	Burgundy wine	250 mL
2	beef bouillon cubes	2
dash	freshly ground pepper	dash

- Combine meat, crumbs, onion, cornstarch, allspice, egg, cream and ¾ tsp. (3 mL) salt; shape into approximately 30 small balls.
- Heat vegetable oil in large skillet and sauté meatballs, a few at a time, until a golden brown color. Remove and keep warm.
- Blend flour with remaining oil in skillet. Add water, wine, bouillon cubes, ½ tsp. (2 mL) salt and pepper. Cook, stirring until smooth.
- Arrange meatballs in sauce; cover and simmer for approximately 30 minutes.
- Serves 4.
- See photograph opposite.

Burgundy Meatballs, page 80

BEAUREGARD TOWN BEEF

Some would say 'meatballs'. Others, like the originator of this recipe, captured the imagination of all and exclaimed, 'tonight we shall have Beauregard Town Beef'.
Sounds great . . . but what is it? Curious? Please . . . read on!

2 lbs.	*leanest ground beef	1 kg
4¼ oz.	can devilled ham	130 g
½ tsp.	salt	2 mL
½ tsp.	garlic salt	2 mL
¼ tsp.	freshly ground pepper	1 mL
½ cup	ketchup	125 mL
½ cup	fine, dry bread crumbs	125 mL
4 tsp.	horseradish	20 mL
2	eggs, lightly beaten	2

- In a large bowl combine all the above ingredients, shape into approximately 40 balls and place on 2 greased baking sheets about 1½" (4 cm) apart.
- Bake for 15-20 minutes at 425°F (240°C). Transfer to chafing or warming dish and serve, 'free choice', with wine sauce and/or buttermilk sauce (below).

WINE SAUCE

2 x 7½ oz.	can tomato sauce	2 x 213 g
½ cup	dry red wine	125 mL
2 tbsp.	sugar	30 mL

- Combine all ingredients and heat, stirring, until barely boiling. Serve in a small container.

BUTTERMILK SAUCE

1¾ cups	buttermilk	425 mL
1 cup	diced processed Swiss cheese	250 g
2 tsp.	cornstarch	10 mL
dash	freshly ground pepper	dash
¾ tsp.	dry mustard	3 mL
6 drops	Tabasco	6 drops

- Combine all ingredients in top of double boiler and cook, stirring, until somewhat thickened. Serve in a small container.
- Now that you know what Beauregard Town Beef is, wait until you taste it, especially with the buttermilk sauce! What an unexpected taste treat, guaranteed to become a long-standing family favorite!
- Serves 4-6.

SOUR CREAM MEATBALLS

Different? Yes. Unusual? Yes. Bound to please? Yes. Especially if you fancy the flavor of sour cream.

1 lb.	*lean ground beef	500 g
¼ cup	sour cream	50 mL
1½ tbsp.	onion soup mix	22 mL
1	egg, slightly beaten	1
3¼ cups	bread crumbs	800 mL
3 tbsp.	flour	45 mL
1½ tsp.	paprika	7 mL
2 tbsp.	butter	30 mL

- Combine hamburger, sour cream, onion soup mix, egg and bread crumbs. Mix thoroughly.
- Roll meatballs in a mixture of flour and paprika, thoroughly coating.
- In medium skillet sauté meatballs in butter.

SAUCE

1	beef bouillon cube	1
1 cup	boiling water	250 mL
1	cream of chicken soup	1
¾ cup	water	175 mL

- Crumble bouillon cube into 1 cup (250 mL) boiling water. Combine with cream of chicken soup and an additional ¾ cup (175 mL) water.
- Pour sauce over meatballs in skillet. Simmer over low heat for 30-35 minutes.
- Serves 2-4.

PINEAPPLE MEATBALLS

Pineapple Meatballs are a great make-ahead-and-freeze recipe. Get everyone's taste buds jumping with a memorable Caesar Salad, page 150, mixed with millions of garlic croûtons. Don't forget to throw in a little grated Parmesan cheese.

Serve these delicious meatballs with white rice, bread sticks and a side dish of snow peas or asparagus. What better way to end your busy day than with coffee or tea and a super easy Butter Tart Slice, page 166, dessert!

1½ lb.	*lean ground beef	750 g
1	small garlic clove, crushed	1
1 tsp.	salt	5 mL
¼ tsp.	pepper	1 mL
3 tbsp.	vegetable cooking oil	45 mL
½ cup	chicken stock (1 chicken bouillon cube in boiling water)	125 mL
2	green peppers, cubed	2
14 oz.	can pineapple chunks, drained, juice reserved	398 mL
3 tbsp.	cornstarch	45 mL
½ cup	sugar	125 mL
½ cup	pineapple juice from can	125 mL
½ cup	vinegar	125 mL
3 tbsp.	soy sauce	45 mL
1	tomato, chopped	1

- Combine beef, garlic, salt and pepper. Shape into medium-small meatballs. Heat small amount of oil in frying pan and slowly cook meatballs to brown evenly on all sides. Remove meatballs as they are cooked.
- Remove all oil but 1 tbsp. (15 mL) and then add chicken bouillon, green pepper and pineapple chunks to pan. Cover and simmer for 5 minutes. Return meatballs to frying pan and cook for an additional 3 minutes.
- Mix cornstarch, sugar, pineapple juice, vinegar and soy sauce together until smooth. Add meatballs to pan, stirring constantly, until sauce thickens. Add chopped tomatoes.
- The different textures and 'crunchiness' of ingredients in this recipe are sure to tease your taste buds!
- Serves 6-8.

KEFTA MKAOUARA

MOROCCAN MEATBALL, TOMATO AND EGG STEW

Imagine passing through an exquisite, arabesque gateway into the city of Fez, once the thriving capital of Morocco. Imagine the adventure of shopping for the ingredients for Kefta in a covered street in the Souks, the marketplace in Fez. Imagine stepping through an arcade to encounter a snake charmer, resplendent in flowing black robes, demonstrating the concentration that ensures that his faithful audience respectfully maintains a 'comfortable' distance from the uniquely patterned reptiles.

On the other hand, shopping for Kefta ingredients in Canada sounds not so bad!

1 lb.	*lean ground beef	500 g
2 tbsp.	chopped fresh parsley	30 mL
1½ tsp.	ground coriander	7 mL
½ tsp.	ground cumin seed	2 mL
1	small onion grated	1
¼ tsp.	cayenne pepper	1 mL
pinch	chili pepper	pinch
pinch	salt	pinch
2 tbsp.	vegetable oil	30 mL
6	eggs	6

SPICY TOMATO SAUCE

2	medium onions, chopped	2
1 bunch	parsley, chopped	1 bunch
2-2½ lbs.	tomatoes, peeled, seeded and chopped	1 kg
1 tsp.	ground cumin	5 mL
1 tsp.	freshly ground pepper	5 mL
2	garlic cloves, chopped	2
½ tsp.	ground cinnamon	2 mL
¼ tsp.	cayenne pepper	1 mL

- Combine all the kefta ingredients except the oil and eggs. Form 1" (2.5 cm) balls. Heat the oil in a frying pan and brown the meatballs on all sides. Remove from pan and set aside, covered.
- Add all the sauce ingredients to the frying pan. Cook for 30 minutes, uncovered, or until the sauce has reduced to a thick gravy. Return the meatballs to the sauce. Cook for an additional 10 minutes.
- Carefully break the eggs into the sauce and poach them until firm. Serve this dish directly from the pan.
- Serves 5-6.

SOUTH AFRICAN BOBOTIE

Feeling adventurous? If so, you will certainly be a big winner with this serving of beef. The flavors found in Bobotie are complemented and enhanced by Yellow Rice. Sliced cucumbers marinated in vinegar and seasoned with salt and pepper offer a refreshing and cleansing taste experience. Thus, Bobotie, served with a green vegetable, will be spectacular on your dinner table!

2 lbs.	*lean ground beef	1 kg
2	finely chopped onions	2
1	apple, diced	1
2 tbsp.	butter	30 mL
2 slices	bread, soaked and squeezed dry	2 slices
2 tbsp.	curry powder	30 mL
2 tbsp.	sugar	30 mL
2	eggs	2
2 tbsp.	vinegar	30 mL
2 tsp.	salt	10 mL
¼ tsp.	pepper	1 mL
¼ cup	raisins	50 mL
12	blanched almonds, quartered	12
4	bay leaves	4
1 cup	milk	250 mL
1 tsp.	turmeric	5 mL

- Sauté onions and apples in butter.
- In a large bowl mix meat, bread, curry powder, sugar, 1 egg, vinegar, salt, pepper, raisins and almonds. Add onions and apples. Place in greased casserole dish. Add bay leaves.
- Bake in 350°F (180°C) oven for 1½ hours. Remove bay leaves.
- Beat 1 egg with milk and pour over Bobotie about 10 minutes before removing from the oven.
- Serve with Yellow Rice, page 160, and chutney.
- Serves 4-6.

BURGUNDY BEEF STEW

The addition of a dry red wine to the gravy accompanying this dish certainly leads to temptation. Subtle flavor and the beefy aroma of gravy, steeped around vegetables deluxe, encourages one to plead, as did Dickens' Oliver, 'Please sir, I want some more'. Delicious little beef bits left behind can only be enjoyed by using a sopping 'soak-it' or 'sippet', page 155.

1 lb.	*lean ground beef	500 g
1 cup	crackers, finely ground	250 g
¼ cup	finely chopped onion	50 mL
1	garlic clove, minced	1
1	egg, lightly beaten	1
1½ tsp.	salt	7 mL
¼ tsp.	freshly ground pepper	1 mL
¼ tsp.	thyme	1 mL
1 tbsp.	butter	15 mL
1 tbsp.	oil	15 mL
1¼ cups	tomato sauce	300 mL
1¼ cups	beef bouillon (page 148)	300 mL
1 cup	dry red wine	250 mL
16	tiny white onions, peeled	16
2	garlic cloves, minced	2
4	medium potatoes, peeled, quartered	4
4	medium carrots, cut in 1'' (2.5 cm) chunks	4
2 stalks	celery, in thick slices	2 stalks
	salt and pepper	
½ lb.	small, fresh mushrooms	250 g
	chopped parsley	
1 cup	water	250 mL
1 tbsp.	cornstarch	15 mL
1½ cups	water	375 mL

- Combine beef, crumbs, chopped onion, garlic, egg, salt, pepper and thyme. Shape into 1½'' (4 cm) meatballs.
- Heat butter and oil in large skillet or Dutch oven. Brown meatballs on all sides. Remove any excess fat.
- Combine remaining ingredients with meatballs in Dutch oven or heavy casserole. Add 1 cup (250 mL) water.
- Cover and bake at 350°F (180°C) for about 45 minutes, or until vegetables are tender. Taste and adjust seasonings.
- Add cornstarch to 1½ cups (375 mL) cold water. Add this to thicken stew.
- Reduce oven heat to 200°F (100°C) and allow stew to simmer and mellow for an additional hour. Add a little water if necessary. Garnish with parsley.
- Serves 6-8.

PORCUPINE BALLS

An extremely easy, quick and delicious recipe which has the potential to serve as an entrée for your family or if you form the meat into smaller balls, as an appetizer.

The flavor and taste of porcupine balls will be complemented if you serve it with a crisp vegetable side dish such as asparagus, Brussels sprouts or even broccoli. Don't overlook the welcome taste of whole-wheat buns snuggled under a wrapper to keep them warm for the dinner table.

A simple and unadorned jellied salad is always a welcome treat. If you listen to the comments generated from such an easy menu, you will wonder why you don't serve it more frequently.

1 lb.	*lean ground beef	500 g
½ cup	uncooked white rice	125 mL
½ cup	onion, finely chopped	125 mL
1	egg, small	1
¾ tsp.	salt	3 mL
dash	pepper	dash
10 oz.	can tomato soup	284 mL
10 oz.	water (1 soup can)	284 mL

- Mix the beef, rice, onion, egg, salt and pepper. Form into 1½" (4 cm) balls.
- Place in a greased casserole dish and cover with tomato soup which has been diluted with 1 equal can of water. Cover and bake for 1½ hours at 350°F (180°C).
- Porcupine balls derive their name from the rice which, during cooking, swells and pops out to form tiny spines.
- Serves 4.

MOUSSAKA

You mustn't let the length of the directions scare you away from this recipe. It is really quite simple to prepare. Speaking of simple, Moussaka is 'superbly simple' to enjoy, again and again. An oil and vinegar dressing tossed with a green salad would leave your dinner companions feeling quite satisfied. A little extra? Try a scoop of ice cream topped with a pear, cut side nestled into the ice cream onto which you pour a hot chocolate sauce. What a meal!!!

1	large eggplant	1
½ cup	flour	125 mL
dash	salt	dash
	oil	

MEAT SAUCE

2 lbs.	*lean ground beef	1 kg
2	medium onions	2
19 oz.	can tomatoes	540 mL
½ cup	dry red wine	125 mL
¼ cup	freshly brewed strong coffee	50 mL
1 tbsp.	parsley flakes	15 mL
1 tsp.	salt	5 mL
1	small garlic clove, minced	1
¼ tsp.	pepper	1 mL
½ tsp.	oregano	2 mL
½ tsp.	cinnamon	2 mL
½ tsp.	rosemary	2 mL
¼ tsp.	nutmeg	1 mL

BÉCHAMEL SAUCE

¼ cup	butter	50 mL
¼ cup	flour	50 mL
¼ tsp.	salt	1 mL
2 cups	milk	500 mL
2	eggs, beaten	2
½ cup	ricotta cheese	125 mL

TOPPING

¾ cup	dry bread crumbs	175 mL
½ cup	grated Parmesan cheese	125 mL

MOUSSAKA (CONT'D.)

- TO PREPARE EGGPLANT, peel and cut into ½" (1 cm) slices, sprinkle with salt and let stand 15 minutes. Wipe slices dry with paper towels. Coat slices in flour and salt mixture. Brown in oil and set aside.
- TO PREPARE MEAT SAUCE, brown beef for meat sauce. Add onions, and cook until tender. Remove excess fat. Add tomatoes, wine, coffee and seasonings. Simmer uncovered until liquid disappears and sauce is thick.
- TO PREPARE BÉCHAMEL SAUCE, melt butter, blend in flour and salt and whisk vigorously until smooth. Remove from heat and slowly add milk, stirring constantly. Return to moderate heat and cook 5 minutes, stirring often. In a small bowl, beat eggs and add ricotta cheese. Blend well and add to béchamel sauce. Return to heat for 1 minute. Remove and set aside.
  Combine bread crumbs with grated Parmesan cheese.
- TO PREPARE MOUSSAKA, grease 9" x 13" x 2" (4 L) baking dish. Arrange ½ the eggplant on the bottom. Sprinkle with ⅓ crumb mixture. Add ½ of meat sauce, smooth and cover with another ⅓ of crumb mixture. With remaining eggplant make another layer, topped with remainder of meat sauce.

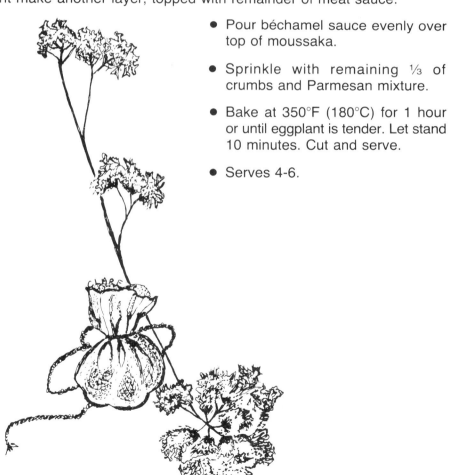

- Pour béchamel sauce evenly over top of moussaka.

- Sprinkle with remaining ⅓ of crumbs and Parmesan mixture.

- Bake at 350°F (180°C) for 1 hour or until eggplant is tender. Let stand 10 minutes. Cut and serve.

- Serves 4-6.

CABBAGE PATCH AND SOUR CREAM

Such a classic, old-fashioned favorite. Great taste, ease of preparation, relatively inexpensive to make, all contribute to the universality of this dish.
If you prefer a bit of zip, try the mustard sauce!

1 lb.	*lean ground beef	500 g
¼ cup	Italian sausage, thinly sliced	50 mL
1	large green cabbage	1
1	small onion, finely chopped	1
1	garlic clove, minced	1
1	carrot, grated	1
⅓ cup	celery, very thinly sliced	75 mL
¼ lb.	mushrooms, chopped	125 g
1 cup	soft bread crumbs	250 mL
¼ cup	dry sherry	50 mL
1 tsp.	salt	5 mL
½ tsp.	dried thyme	2 mL
¼ tsp.	freshly ground pepper	1 mL
1 tbsp.	caraway seeds	15 mL
3	slices bacon	3
2 cups	chicken bouillon, (dissolve 2 chicken bouillon cubes in 2 cups (500 mL) boiling water)	500 mL

- Cut slice from core end of cabbage and remove core. Cut out inside of cabbage, leaving 1" (2.5 cm) shell.
- In a deep saucepan, cover cabbage shell with boiling water. Cover and cook about 10 minutes until still crisp but slightly tender.
- Remove and invert cabbage to drain well. Remove 1 large outer leaf and set aside.
- Combine beef, Italian sausage, onion, garlic, carrot, celery, mushrooms, crumbs, sherry, salt, thyme, pepper and caraway seeds in a large bowl. Spoon mixture into hollowed cabbage.
- Line bottom of heavy covered casserole or Dutch oven with bacon, place cabbage on top. Cover beef filling with reserved cabbage leaf. Pour chicken bouillon into casserole, cover and bring to a boil. Reduce heat and simmer for 1½ hours or until filling is cooked.
- Serves 4-6.

  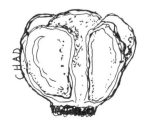

MUSTARD SAUCE (FOR CABBAGE PATCH)

2 tbsp.	butter	30 mL
2 tbsp.	all-purpose flour	30 mL
1¼ cups	hot cooking broth from cabbage	300 mL
1½ tsp.	Dijon-style mustard	7 mL
2 tbsp.	fresh, finely chopped parsley	30 mL
dash	freshly grated nutmeg	dash

- In a small saucepan, melt butter, stir in flour and cook over medium heat for 1 minute. Pour in hot broth and whisk until thickened and cooked, about 2 minutes. Whisk in mustard, parsley and nutmeg to taste.

SUPER SKILLET SUPPER

An easily prepared dinner. One that allows for even the cook to join in the softball game, as a combination manager, pitcher and umpire. Never heard of that combination? Come play on our team. Did we ever mention the final score?

1 lb.	*lean ground beef	500 g
2 x 19 oz.	cans tomatoes	2 x 540 mL
½ cup	chopped green pepper	125 mL
½ cup	chopped celery	125 mL
½ cup	chopped onions	125 mL
1 cup	canned corn kernels	250 mL
½ cup	uncooked white rice	125 mL
½ cup	barbecue sauce	125 mL
¼ cup	Worcestershire sauce	50 mL
½ tsp.	salt	2 mL
½ cup	peas, frozen	125 g
8 oz.	sliced Cheddar cheese	250 g

- In a large heavy skillet, brown beef. Remove any excess fat.
- Add tomatoes, green peppers, celery, onions, corn, rice, barbecue sauce, Worcestershire sauce and salt. Cover and simmer for 25 minutes, stirring occasionally.
- Add frozen peas during last 7 minutes of cooking.
- Top with Cheddar cheese cut into triangles. Momentarily cover skillet to allow cheese to melt.
- Serves 6 and the manager gets a 'walk'.

CAMPANA PEPPERS — STUFFED

Extravagantly colorful to serve and guaranteed to become a frequent . . . "Mom, when are you going to make stuffed peppers again?"

Although the directions look lengthy . . . please don't fuss because they really are quite simple and do not take much time.

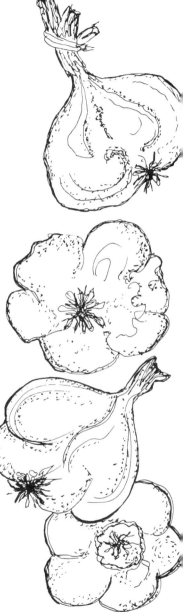

1 lb.	*ground beef, not too lean	500 g
¼ cup	vegetable oil	50 mL
⅓ cup	long-grain rice	75 mL
1	large onion, finely chopped	1
3	garlic cloves, finely chopped	3
⅛ tsp.	Italian seasoning	0.5 mL
½ cup	beef bouillon, (page 148)	125 mL
2¾ lbs.	tomatoes, ripe	1.3 kg
dash	salt	dash
dash	freshly ground pepper	dash
½ tsp.	freshly chopped parsley	2 mL
1 tbsp.	drained capers	15 mL
4	bell (in Spain, we would shop for campana) peppers — 2 green, 1 yellow, 1 red, equal-sized	4
⅔ cup	tomato paste	150 mL
pinch	sugar	sugar
	dry red wine, if needed to lighten sauce	
½ tsp.	chopped basil	2 mL

- In large saucepan heat vegetable oil. Add rice and stir over high heat until transparent. Add half the onion and half the garlic and sauté until they are also transparent. Add meat and cook until brown.
- Add beef bouillon, Italian seasoning and scrape up browned bits from bottom of pan. Bring to boil, then cover and simmer over low heat until rice is nearly cooked, about 10 minutes. Do not overcook rice at this point.
- Immerse tomatoes in boiling water — let stand for 1 minute. Transfer to cold water. Peel and halve the tomatoes. Thinly slice 2 tomato halves for filling; dice remaining tomatoes.

- Season meat mixture with salt and pepper. Taste and adjust seasoning if necessary.
- Mix parsley, capers and thinly sliced tomato into meat.
- Starting just below the stem end, cut horizontally across each pepper to form a lid . . . good practice for Halloween pumpkins! Clean inside, rinse and pat dry. Stuff peppers with meat mixture and cover with pepper 'lids.' Set aside.

TOMATO SAUCE

- Heat 1 tbsp. (15 mL) vegetable oil in large saucepan. Add remaining onion and garlic and sauté for 5 minutes. Stir in diced tomatoes and tomato paste. Season with salt, freshly ground pepper and sugar. Cover and simmer over low heat for 10 minutes, adding a bit of dry red wine if sauce becomes too thick. Taste and adjust seasoning again if necessary.
- Place stuffed peppers in sauce, cover and cook for 40 minutes over low heat.
- Remove peppers. Keep warm. Purée or strain sauce and reheat. Stir in basil. Serve peppers in sauce, accompanied by a vegetable side dish and a smartly seasoned oil and vinegar dressing poured over a green salad loaded with crunchy croûtons.
- Want to drive your eating public absolutely crazy? Somehow find the time to whip up the best ever, most fantastic, simply wonderful . . . Mississippi Mud! page 168.
- Serves 4.

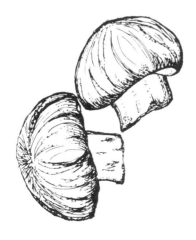

ONION SCOOPS

By any chance do you have a big appetite that sits down to your table from time to time? Does your appetite appreciate a fine and satisfying serving of beef? Then try onion scoops.

Warm, whole-wheat dinner rolls, a fresh garden vegetable and Tomatoes with Horseradish Sauce, page 156, is almost too much for one sitting.

A special little treat for dessert . . . don't overlook the fun of fortune cookies. And there is nothing stopping you from slipping a message from the chef into one or all of the cookies.

Coffee . . . have you ever tried adding ¼ tsp. (1 mL) of cinnamon to ground coffee? What a gratifying finish to a long and busy day!

½ lb.	*lean ground beef	250 g
8	large yellow onions	8
1 cup	canned tomatoes, undrained	250 mL
½ cup	finely chopped green pepper	125 mL
¼ cup	fine, dry bread crumbs	50 mL
3 tbsp.	chopped raisins	45 mL
2 tbsp.	slivered almonds	30 mL
1	garlic clove, minced	1
2 tsp.	red wine	10 mL
½ tsp.	salt	2 mL
¼ tsp.	cinnamon	1 mL
dash	pepper	dash
1 cup	beef bouillon, (page 148)	250 mL
½ cup	water	125 mL

- Peel onions. Slice off tops, scoop out and reserve centers, leaving shells about 1'' (2.5 cm) thick. Finely chop onion centers to obtain 1 cup (250 mL) onions.
- Cook onion shells for about 5 minutes in a large saucepan of lightly salted boiling water. Remove and invert onion shells on paper towels to drain.
- In large skillet sauté beef. Add 1 cup (250 mL) chopped onion and cook for 5 minutes.
- Drain and chop tomatoes, reserving juice and add tomatoes to skillet along with green pepper, cook 5 minutes longer. Stir in bread crumbs, raisins, almonds, garlic, wine, salt, cinnamon and pepper, cook for 5 minutes.
- Arrange onion shells in casserole large enough to accommodate onions in single layer. Evenly divide and spoon meat mixture into onion shells.
- Combine reserved juice from tomatoes, beef bouillon and water in a large saucepan; heat to boiling. Pour into casserole to depth of 1'' (2.5 cm).
- Bake for 35-40 minutes at 350°F (180°C) or until onions are tender.
- Arrange on serving platter and spoon juices over top. Garnish onion scoops with fresh parsley.
- Serves 4.

MEATBALL STEW WITH SPINACH DUMPLINGS

Do you suppose ol' Popeye had any idea that his favorite 'up and at 'em' would be as popular and widely used, as is the case today?

The delicate and enhancing flavor of spinach has found its way into many traditional and contemporary recipes, and we think that this is certainly one of the best.

1 lb.	*lean ground beef	500 g
1	egg, slightly beaten	1
¾ cup	soft bread crumbs	175 mL
½ tsp.	garlic clove, minced	2 mL
½ tsp.	salt	2 mL
¼ tsp.	pepper	1 mL
1 tbsp.	vegetable oil	15 mL
1	medium onion, chopped	1
10 oz.	can Cheddar cheese soup condensed	284 mL
1¼ cups	milk	300 mL
14 oz.	can diced beets, drained	398 mL
10½ oz.	Brussels sprouts, frozen	300 g
¼ cup	thinly sliced celery	50 mL
8 oz.	frozen spinach, well thawed, drained and chopped	250 g
1 cup	tea biscuit mix	250 mL
¼ cup	milk	50 mL

- Mix egg, crumbs, garlic, salt and pepper. Add beef and mix well.
- Shape meat mixture into 1" (2.5 cm) meatballs. Heat oil in large skillet and brown meatballs evenly on all sides. Add onions and cook 5 minutes. Remove any excess fat.
- Combine cheese soup and milk; add to skillet. Cover and simmer for 10 minutes. Add beets and sprouts. Cover and simmer for 5 minutes.
- Stir together spinach, tea biscuit mix and ¼ cup (50 mL) milk. Drop spinach mixture atop stew to make 8 dumplings. Cover and simmer 10 minutes.
- Serves 4.

STUFFED CABBAGE ROLLS

The subtle flavor of cabbage rolls is what makes generation after generation succumb to its flavor. Serve sippets, page 155, to mop up the delicious bits and pieces!

For dessert . . . a gentle ORANGE MOUSSE, page 166, with a sugar wafer tucked along the side of the serving dish.

2 lbs.	*lean ground beef	1 kg
1	large cabbage	1
1½ tbsp.	butter	22 mL
1½ tbsp.	olive oil	22 mL
½	medium onion, finely chopped	½
¼ cup	leek, finely chopped	50 mL
1	garlic clove, finely minced	1
1½ cup	cooked rice	375 mL
3 tbsp.	finely minced parsley	45 mL
½ tsp.	thyme	2 mL
1 tsp.	salt	5 mL
¼ tsp.	freshly ground pepper	1 mL
¼ cup	Italian sausage, thinly sliced	50 mL
1 cup	beef bouillon (page 148)	250 mL
1 cup	tomato sauce	250 mL
¼ cup	dry sherry	50 mL
1	bay leaf	1

- Prepare the cabbage by peeling off the rough outer leaves. Cut out the bottom core of the head with a paring knife. Place in a large pot filled with boiling, salted water. Boil covered for 5 minutes or until leaves separate easily. Invert and drain. Separate the individual leaves and pat dry.
- In a frying pan heat butter and oil, add onion, leek and garlic; sauté until onion is transparent. Add meat and brown. Remove any excess fat. Add rice, parsley, salt, thyme, pepper and Italian sausage. Mix well.
- Fill each leaf with 2-3 tbsp. (30-45 mL) of stuffing. Wrap the leaf around the filling and place the roll, sealed side down, in a casserole dish.
- Combine the bouillon, tomato sauce, sherry and bay leaf. Pour over the rolls in the casserole dish. Cover and bake 1 hour, adding more liquid if needed.
- Remove bay leaf before serving.
- Serves 8.
- P.S. This recipe is 'freezer friendly.'

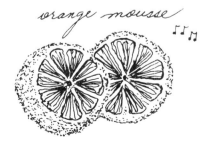

orange mousse

BEEF TACOS

'Hey Mom, the guys are coming back with me after hockey practice. Okay? Gee thanks, Mom.' It is said that the best defense is a good offense. Now the guys listening might have thought I had time to answer, but I didn't. Anyhow, who could possibly resist the camaraderie generated among 6 young men (teen-agers) wearing various sizes and shapes of baggy, frayed, slightly less than clean and fresh 'sweats'. Even the oppressive odors radiating from their runners don't stop them at the back door as they burst through asking, 'what did you make?'

What else, who can resist the spices and flavor of Mexico? Not this crew. TACOS! GREAT!

1 lb.	*lean ground beef	500 g
½ cup	chopped onion	125 mL
½ cup	chopped green pepper	125 mL
1 tsp.	chili powder	5 mL
1 tsp.	Worcestershire sauce	5 mL
dash	Tabasco	dash
½ tsp.	garlic salt	2 mL
½ tsp.	sugar	2 mL
¼ tsp.	dry mustard	1 mL
2 tbsp.	ketchup	30 mL
	taco shells	
	shredded lettuce	
	chopped tomatoes	
	grated Cheddar cheese	
	chili or taco sauce	
	sour cream	

- In skillet brown ground beef, remove any excess fat. Add onions and green peppers, sauté for 3 minutes.
- Stir in chili powder, Worcestershire sauce, Tabasco, garlic, salt, sugar, dry mustard and ketchup. Bring to a boil, reduce heat. Simmer, uncovered, until thickened, about 15-20 minutes.
- Fill each taco shell with about 2 tbsp. (30 mL) beef filling. Top beef with lettuce, tomatoes, olives and cheese. Pass the chili or taco sauce and sour cream to top individual tacos.
- Serves 6.

MEXICAN BURRITOS

Fantastico, means the same in any language. Fantastic food from sunny Mexico where little donkeys, **Burritos,** *are super easy to make and so scrumptious that they will disappear faster than you can pronounce their name!*

½ lb.	*lean ground beef	250 g
1	garlic clove, minced	1
2 tbsp.	finely minced onions	30 mL
14 oz.	can pork and beans	398 mL
3 tbsp.	ketchup	45 mL
1 tsp.	vinegar	5 mL
½ tsp.	chili powder	2 mL
½ tsp.	freshly ground pepper	2 mL
¼ tsp.	cinnamon	1 mL
½ tsp.	salt	2 mL
	tortillas, see below	
	tomato, cheese and shredded lettuce	
	sour cream	

- Combine beef, garlic and onion in a skillet; cook until meat is browned. Add the pork and beans, ketchup, vinegar, chili powder, pepper, cinnamon and salt.
- Cook over medium heat for about 10 minutes or until some of the moisture has evaporated.

CORN TORTILLAS, soft tortillas to wrap around our mildly spiced meat filling.

2 cups	instant corn masa (finely ground corn)	500 mL
½ tsp.	salt	2 mL
1 cup	warm water	250 mL

- Combine corn masa and salt. Gradually add water until dough is just moist enough to hold together. Compress dough into small ball and knead a few times until smooth.
- Divide and shape dough into 12 small balls. Place each ball between waxed paper and roll into a 5½" (14 cm) circle. Leave between paper until all are rolled.
- Remove top paper and invert tortilla onto ungreased skillet over medium heat. Remove bottom sheet and cook for 30 seconds. Turn; press gently with pancake flipper until bubbles form in tortilla. Turn again; cook 1 minute longer or until bottom of tortilla has small brown spots.
- Remove tortilla; stack and wrap in foil to keep warm.
- Place 2 tbsp. (30 mL) of the meat filling on each tortilla. Sprinkle with chopped tomato, shredded lettuce and cheese. Simply roll up and place, seam side down, on a serving platter.

MEXICAN BURRITOS (CONT'D.)

- Aaahh!! the topping — a scrumptious, light, tart tasting dollop of sour cream. Complement your Burrito with a serving of Spanish rice and a green salad topped off with a mellow dressing.
- Makes 12 Burritos or 6 servings.
- Push your chairs back and over coffee with fresh fruit and yogurt, talk away the day!

LA SALSA PERFETTA

THE PERFECT SAUCE

A pasta sauce . . . the likes of which you've never tasted. A spicy sauce, perfect for serving with your favorite family pasta.

A full-bodied red wine, a fresh garden salad and crusty French bread, everything possible for a relaxing and fulfilling meal!

2 lbs	*lean ground beef	1 kg
2 lbs.	hot Italian sausage	1 kg
½ cup	unsalted butter	125 mL
1	large onion, coarsely chopped	1
1	green pepper, diced	1
2 stalks	celery, diced	2 stalks
3 x 19 oz.	cans tomatoes	3 x 540 mL
1	bay leaf	1
3 tbsp.	dried oregano	45 mL
2 tbsp.	dried basil	30 mL
dash	Italian seasoning	dash
½ tsp.	paprika	2 mL
2 tsp.	salt	10 mL
1 tsp.	pepper, freshly ground	5 mL
1 cup	dry red wine	250 mL
2 x 5½ oz.	cans tomato paste	2 x 156 mL
1 tsp.	sugar	5 mL

- Cut the sausage into ½" (1 cm) cubes and brown in a heavy skillet over medium heat. Drain and set aside.
- Sauté the ground beef in same skillet over medium heat and set aside.
- Melt the butter in a large saucepan over medium heat. Sauté the onion, green pepper and celery.
- Stir in sausage, beef, tomatoes with liquid, bay leaf, oregano, basil, Italian seasoning, paprika, salt and pepper. Simmer covered for 1 hour. Stir in the wine, tomato paste, and sugar. Simmer covered for 2 hours.
- Serves 6-8.
- See photograph, page 112.

BOLOGNESE MEAT SAUCE

Italian cuisine has, for many years now, been a favorite of most North Americans.

Superb pastas made from Durum wheat (probably grown in Canada) come in many sizes and shapes. Long thin pastas, such as spaghetti, fettuccini, and linguine are often topped with sauces.

And the sauce of sauces is BOLOGNESE, beef-filled and bountiful!

1½ lbs.	*lean ground beef	750 g
3 slices	bacon, cooked	3 slices
2 x 14 oz.	cans tomatoes, cut up	2 x 398 mL
1 cup	chopped onions	250 mL
¼ cup	finely chopped carrot	50 mL
¼ cup	finely chopped celery	50 mL
¼ cup	finely snipped parsley	50 mL
¼ cup	tomato paste	50 mL
½ tsp.	instant chicken bouillon granules	2 mL
1 tsp.	salt	5 mL
¼ tsp.	freshly ground pepper	1 mL
⅛ tsp.	ground nutmeg	0.5 mL
1 tsp.	dried oregano	5 mL
½ tsp.	dried basil	2 mL
½ cup	dry white wine	125 mL
¼ cup	water	50 mL
⅓ cup	light cream or milk	75 mL

- In a Dutch oven or large saucepan cook bacon until crisp. Add ground beef and cook until meat is browned. Remove excess fat.
- Add undrained tomatoes, onion, carrot, celery, parsley, tomato paste, bouillon granules, salt, pepper, nutmeg, oregano and basil to meat mixture.
- Stir in wine and water. Bring to a boil.
- Reduce heat and boil very gently, uncovered for 45-60 minutes or until desired thickness. Stir occasionally.
- Just before serving add cream or milk to the sauce.
- Serve immediately with pasta and pass along grated Parmesan cheese.
- Serves 4-6.

LASAGNE FLORENTINE

Lasagne is a beef dish that can be served time and time again. One might think that frequent servings would wear thin. However, detailed research in our family over the years has determined that this is not the case. Lasagne continues to win friends and 'brownie points'.

2 lbs.	*lean ground beef	1 kg
10 oz.	spinach, fresh or frozen	285 g
1 cup	finely chopped onion	250 mL
2	garlic cloves, crushed	2
¾ tsp.	dried basil leaves	3 mL
½ tsp.	oregano leaves	2 mL
½ leaf	bay leaf	½ leaf
19 oz.	tomatoes	540 mL
14 oz.	tomato sauce	398 mL
5½ oz.	tomato paste	156 mL
1½ tsp.	salt	7 mL
⅛ tsp.	freshly ground pepper	0.5 mL
2 tbsp.	minced parsley	30 mL
½ lb.	lasagne noodles (approx. 9 noodles)	250 g
2 cups	2% cottage cheese	500 mL
2 cups	mozzarella cheese	500 mL

- If spinach is frozen, drain and pat dry with paper towels.
- Sauté over medium heat, ground beef, onion, garlic, basil, oregano and bay leaf. Add tomatoes, tomato sauce, tomato paste, salt, pepper and parsley, mix well, mashing tomatoes with fork.
- Bring to boil. Reduce heat, simmer uncovered for 3 hours. Stir occasionally. Remove from heat.
- Preheat oven to 325°F (160°C). Cook lasagne noodles according to package directions, drain thoroughly. Grease a 9" x 13" (22 x 33 cm) casserole dish.
- Layer in the casserole dish: half the noodles, half the meat sauce, half the spinach, repeat layers.
- Spoon low-fat cottage cheese over the Lasagne Florentine.
- Finally, completely cover this unbelievably delicious dinner with grated mozzarella cheese.
- Cover with foil, tucking around the edge.
- Bake 40 minutes; remove foil, bake uncovered for an additional 20 minutes, or until bubbly. Cool for 10 minutes before serving.
- Serves 8.

CANNELLONI

BRAVO! BRAVO! A smooth, mellow, delicious meat filling snuggled into manicotti shells, covered with a white béchamel sauce then with a tomato sauce.

ENCORE! ENCORE! Truth wins out, Cannelloni is a tough act to follow. There is absolutely no question that you will be hard pressed to surpass this beef serving in subsequent meals.

Cannelloni demands nothing less than a Caesar salad, page 150, hot crusty garlic bread, a fruity, fun-flavored, Hungarian wine like Egri Bikavek and good friends to share a feast!

TOMATO SAUCE

2 tbsp.	olive oil	30 mL
1 cup	finely chopped onion	250 mL
4 cups	canned tomatoes, not drained	1 L
6 tbsp.	tomato paste	90 mL
2 tbsp.	basil, fresh OR	30 mL
2 tsp.	basil, dried	10 mL
2 tsp.	sugar	10 mL
1 tsp.	salt	5 mL
to taste	pepper	to taste

- Heat oil, add onion and cook until soft. Add tomatoes and remaining ingredients. Reduce heat and simmer for about 45 minutes.

FILLING

1 lb.	*lean ground beef	500 g
2 tbsp.	olive oil	30 mL
¼ cup	finely chopped onion	50 mL
1 tsp.	finely chopped garlic clove	5 mL
10 oz.	frozen spinach OR	283 g
¾ lb.	fresh spinach, cooked	340 g
2 tbsp.	butter	30 mL
5 tbsp.	Parmesan cheese	75 mL
2 tbsp.	heavy cream	30 mL
2	eggs	2
½ tsp.	dried oregano	2 mL
dash	salt	dash
dash	pepper	dash

CANNELLONI (CONT'D.)

- In large skillet heat oil, add the onion and garlic and cook until soft. Add spinach and cook several minutes longer until moisture evaporates. Remove mixture to separate bowl.
- Add beef to skillet and brown. Remove any excess fat. Add beef and remaining ingredients to onion and garlic mixture.

PASTA

Cook 12-16 manicotti shells according to package directions.

BÉCHAMEL SAUCE

6 tbsp.	butter	90 mL
6 tbsp.	flour	90 mL
1 cup	milk	250 mL
1 cup	heavy cream	250 mL
1 tsp.	salt	5 mL
⅛ tsp.	pepper	0.5 mL

- Melt butter. Add flour. Slowly add milk and cream. Cook to a boil, stirring constantly. Reduce heat and simmer for 2-3 minutes. Add salt and pepper.

TO ASSEMBLE

- Lightly grease a large casserole dish. Fill pasta shells with beef filling and arrange in rows in casserole. Pour on béchamel sauce and then cover with tomato sauce. Sprinkle lightly with Parmesan cheese.
- Serves 8.

PERIETTO PASTA PIE

A perfect Italian, hearty one-dish meal — unquestionably suited for late autumn. A well-deserved feast after the raking and removal of millions upon millions of delicately colored leaves which somehow found their way to a new home, in your backyard!

Complement Perietto Pasta Pie with a Caesar Salad, page 150, and sesame bread sticks. And since you worked so hard at cleaning up after Mother Nature's gift of summer, you deserve the opening of a lovely bottle of Hermitage, thus enjoying an Australian spring in the fall.

1 lb.	*lean ground beef	500 g
6 oz.	uncooked spaghetti	170 g
2 tbsp.	butter	30 mL
2	eggs, beaten	2
⅓ cup	Parmesan cheese	75 mL
1 cup	cream-style cottage cheese	250 mL
½ cup	chopped onion	125 mL
¼ cup	chopped green pepper	50 mL
8 oz.	can tomatoes, cut up	250 g
5½ oz.	can tomato paste	156 g
1 tsp.	sugar	5 mL
1 tsp.	salt	5 mL
1 tsp.	dried oregano, crushed	5 mL
½ tsp.	garlic salt	2 mL
½ cup	shredded mozzarella cheese	125 mL

- Cook spaghetti as directed. Drain and stir butter into hot spaghetti, stir in eggs and Parmesan cheese. Form spaghetti mixture into a 'crust' in a greased 9'' x 2 '' (22 x 5 cm) pie plate. Spread with cottage cheese.
- Sauté beef in a large skillet until golden brown. Add onion and green pepper and cook until tender. Remove any excess fat. Stir in undrained tomatoes, tomato paste, sugar, salt, oregano and garlic salt; heat through.
- Spoon meat mixture into spaghetti crust. Cover edges with foil. Bake in 350°F (180°C) oven for 20 minutes. Sprinkle with mozzarella cheese, bake an additional 5 minutes more or until cheese is melted.
- Serves 4.

*one for me
two for you*

BEEF 'N' BUTTERFLY PASTA

I lb.	*lean ground beef	500 g
1½ cups	crackers	375 mL
½ cup	chopped onion	125 mL
2	eggs, slightly beaten	2
1 tbsp.	minced, fresh parsley	15 mL
1	garlic clove, pressed	1
1 tsp.	salt	5 mL
¼ tsp.	dried mint	1 mL
dash	freshly ground pepper	dash
dash	cinnamon	dash
1¼ cups	butterfly pasta	300 mL
1½ tsp.	salt	7 mL
1 tsp.	vegetable oil	5 mL

- In a medium bowl, combine beef, crackers, onion, eggs, parsley, garlic, 1 tsp. (5 mL) salt, mint, pepper and cinnamon.
- Heat 1 tbsp. (15 mL) oil for frying in a large skillet. Shape meat mixture into 18 small patties. Coat with flour. Fry over medium heat until brown — about 10 minutes on each side. Reserve 1 tbsp. (15 mL) drippings for sauce. Set patties aside and keep warm. Prepare tomato sauce (below).
- Add salt and oil to rapidly boiling water in a 4-quart (4 L) saucepan. Gradually add uncooked butterfly pasta. Cook pasta until tender but still firm. Drain.
- Place cooked butterfly pasta in a large greased baking dish. Arrange meat patties on top of pasta. Spoon tomato sauce over patties and pasta. Cook at 375°F (190°C) for about 20 minutes. Serve immediately.
- Serves 4-6.

TOMATO SAUCE

14 oz.	can tomato sauce	398 mL
2 tbsp.	finely chopped onions	30 mL
2 tbsp.	finely chopped green pepper	30 mL
2 tbsp.	finely chopped celery	30 mL
½ cup	water	125 mL
1 tbsp.	reserved drippings	15 mL
2 tsp.	butter	10 mL
½ tsp.	salt	2 mL
¼ tsp.	dried oregano	1 mL
½ tsp.	Italian seasoning	2 mL
dash	freshly ground pepper	dash

- In a small saucepan combine all ingredients and heat thoroughly. Makes 2½ cups (625 mL).

BEEF IN MANICOTTI

A smooth, lightly spiced, tomato-flavored beef mixture surrounded by a light fresh pasta tube called manicotti. Pasta aficionados might well prefer a spinach manicotti.

This great recipe is a perfect 'make-ahead'. The meat sauce can be made the day before or the morning of, and stored in the refrigerator. It then only takes a few minutes to complete this 'grumblies over now' meal.

Freshly sliced cucumber smothered in a half and half mixture of white and red wine vinegars, topped with fresh ground pepper and salt offers a crisp palate-pleasing balance to this dish!

1 lb.	*lean ground beef	500 g
8	manicotti shells, plain or spinach	8
2 x 5½ oz.	cans tomato paste	2 x 156 mL
½ cup	chopped onion	125 mL
1	finely grated carrot	1
⅓ cup	snipped parsley	75 mL
1 tbsp.	dried, crushed basil	15 mL
½ tsp.	oregano	2 mL
1½ tsp.	salt	7 mL
dash	pepper	dash
1	large garlic clove, minced	1
2 cups	water	500 mL
2	eggs, beaten	2
3 cups	ricotta cheese	750 mL
½ cup	grated Parmesan cheese	125 mL
¼ tsp.	salt	1 mL

- Cook manicotti shells according to package directions until just tender, drain and rinse with cold water. Meanwhile, in a 3-quart (1.5 L) saucepan brown meat lightly. Remove any excess fat.
- Stir in tomato paste, onion, carrot, ½ of the parsley, basil, oregano, 1½ tsp. (7 mL) salt, garlic and a dash of pepper. Add water and mix well. Simmer uncovered for 15 minutes, stirring occasionally.
- Combine eggs, ricotta cheese, ¼ of the Parmesan cheese, remaining parsley, ¼ tsp. (1 mL) salt and a dash of pepper.
- Stuff the cooked manicotti shells with the cheese mixture using a small spoon. Pour half of the tomato-meat sauce into a baking dish. Arrange stuffed manicotti in dish and top with remaining sauce. Sprinkle with Parmesan cheese.
- Bake uncovered at 350°F (180°C) for 40-45 minutes. Let stand for 10 minutes before serving.
- A marvelous feast which serves 6.

SLUMGULLION

Fortunately Slumgullion offers enough of the 'good stuff,' namely taste, to overcome its name. Additionally, family fun and conversation can be easily generated in speculating about the origins of the name.

Make a real game of it . . . the most outlandish and most speculative explanation is allowed free rein and 'feet up!' Rules of fair play include telling everyone in the morning that Slumgullion is on the menu that evening thus allowing ample time for the fabrication of tall tales.

2 lb.	*lean ground beef	1 kg
1	medium onion, chopped	1
1	green pepper, chopped	1
1 stalk	celery, chopped	1 stalk
¼ lb.	fresh mushrooms, sliced	125 g
1 cup	cubed cheese	250 mL
10 oz.	can tomato soup, undiluted	284 mL
19 oz.	can tomatoes	540 mL
12 oz.	pkg. fettuccini noodles	340 g
¼ cup	butter	50 mL
2 cups	buttered bread cubes (butter each slice of bread first, then cut into ½'' (1 cm) cubes)	500 mL

- Fry meat until lightly browned. Add onions, green pepper and celery; sauté for 2 minutes. Add sliced mushrooms, cheese, tomato soup and canned tomatoes. Simmer 5 minutes.
- Add 2 tbsp. (30 mL) butter or margarine to salted, boiling water in a large pot. Add fettuccini and cook according to package directions.
- Drain through colander or sieve, return noodles to large pot and add ¼ cup (50 mL) butter, tossing gently with fork until butter melts and evenly coats fettuccini.
- Butter a large 3-qt. (3 L) casserole and spoon in alternate layers of noodles and meat mixture until all is used, beginning and ending with fettuccini.
- Top with buttered bread cubes. Bake at 350°F (180°C) uncovered for 1 hour making sure bread cubes are golden and crisp.
- Fresh green peas and a Green Goddess Salad, page 155, will go a long way in helping the less-talented storytellers in your family forget their woes!
- Serves 6-8.

CRÊPES SALTIMBOCCA

Crêpes . . . very much a part of the smart crowd of the 80's! Also an integral part of that same crowd is *LEAN Canadian-produced BEEF. Crêpes Saltimbocca, combining the two, is a unique experience, one that can be thoroughly enjoyed at a Sunday brunch or a TGIF get together. Your TGIF scenario might include an Italian Valpolicella wine.

½ lb.	*lean ground beef	250 g
1	medium onion, finely chopped	1
2 tbsp.	grated Parmesan cheese	30 mL
½ tsp.	ground sage	2 mL
¼ tsp.	dried parsley	1 mL
dash	freshly ground pepper	dash
2 x 3 oz.	pkg. ham, very thinly sliced	2 x 85 g
12	Crêpes, (see recipe below)	12
4 slices	mozzarella cheese	4 slices
2 tbsp.	milk	30 mL
½ cup	sour cream	125 mL
2	green onions, finely chopped	2

- Sauté ground beef and onion until meat is browned. Remove beef from pan with slotted spoon and let rest on paper towelling for a minute or 2.
- Spoon beef into bowl and add Parmesan cheese, sage and parsley.
- Divide ham slices among crêpes, arranging them on unbrowned sides. Cut cheese slices crosswise into thirds. Place 1 piece atop ham on each crêpe. Spoon about 2 tbsp. (30 mL) beef mixture in the center of each.
- Fold 1 side of crêpe on top of the other side overlapping filling. Place seam side down in a greased 9" x 13" x 2" (22 x 33 x 5 cm) baking dish. Cover and refrigerate for 3-24 hours.
- To serve, bake, uncovered, for approximately 35 minutes in a 375°F (190°C) oven.
- Stir milk into sour cream. Stir in green onion and spoon over crêpes.
- Serves 6.

MAKE-AHEAD CRÊPES

1½ cups	milk	375 mL
1 cup	all-purpose flour	250 mL
2	eggs	2
1 tbsp.	vegetable oil	15 mL
¼ tsp.	salt	1 mL

- Combine all ingredients; beat well. Heat greased 6" (15 cm) skillet. Remove skillet from heat and add 2 tbsp. (30 mL) batter; tip skillet to evenly spread the batter. Return to heat; brown on 1 side.

MAKE-AHEAD CRÊPES (CONT'D.)

- Remove crêpe by inverting skillet over paper towelling. Repeat with remaining batter, greasing skillet occasionally.
- Makes 16-18 crêpes.
- Make-ahead crêpes are 'freezer friendly.' Place 2 layers of waxed paper between crêpes. Wrap with moisture-vaporproof bag and place in freezer. Thaw at room temperature 1 hour before using.

BISCUIT BEEF ROLL

A delightful roll, sliced just before serving. Fresh baby carrots, topped with a smidge of butter and brown sugar and a zingy Spinach Salad, page 153, will have your family asking for repeats!

1 lb.	*lean ground beef	500 g
1	medium onion, chopped	1
1 cup	chopped mushrooms	250 mL
¼ cup	beef bouillon (page 148)	50 mL
1 tsp.	salt	5 mL
¼ tsp.	pepper	1 mL
1 tbsp.	Worcestershire sauce	15 mL
2 cups	tea biscuit mix	500 mL
2 tbsp.	Dijon-style mustard	30 mL
½ cup	old Cheddar cheese, grated	125 mL
2 tbsp.	butter	30 mL

- Sauté beef and onions. Add mushrooms and cook for 2 minutes. Remove any excess fat.
- Add beef broth and seasonings. Simmer, uncovered, until liquid evaporates. Allow mixture to cool.
- Prepare tea biscuit mix according to package directions for rolled biscuits. Roll dough to a ¼" (1 cm) thickness in a rectangular shape. Carefully spread thin layer of Dijon-style mustard over dough.
- Spread cooled mixture to within ½" (1.5 cm) of the edge of the dough. Sprinkle meat with grated cheese. Roll up as in a jelly roll. Pinch seam together.
- Bake at 400°F (200°C) for 15 minutes, reduce heat to 350°F (180°C) and bake for another 30 minutes. During the last 15 minutes, melt 2 tbsp. (30 mL) butter and gently paint beef roll with butter.
- Serves 4-6.
- Biscuit Beef Roll is 'freezer friendly"!

MOGUL BREAD FILLED WITH BEEF AND HERBS

Information, and especially the ease of accessing information, has created phenomenal interest in what other cultures are doing, listening to, thinking about, driving, admiring and, of course eating.

Breads from India with a great diversity of fillings and flavors are becoming very popular. When considering the use of breads with other foods, arrive at a careful balance through contrast. If your bread stuffing is strong and spicy, offer a light cool salad.

DOUGH

2 cups	whole-wheat flour	500 mL
1 cup	instant blending flour	250 mL
3 tbsp.	vegetable oil	45 mL
1 cup	very warm water	250 mL
	additional whole-wheat flour for kneading	

- Combine flours and oil in large bowl. Rub with fingertips to distribute oil.
- Slowly mix in water. Gather dough together. Knead until smooth, dusting with flour only if dough becomes sticky, about 5 minutes. Cover and let rise 30 minutes.
- Can be refrigerated for up to 5 days. Before using, return mixture to room temperature.

STUFFING

1 lb.	*lean ground beef	500 g
3 tbsp.	vegetable oil	45 mL
1 tbsp.	ground ginger	15 mL
1 tsp.	garlic salt	5 mL
1½ tsp.	ground cumin	7 mL
1½ tsp.	curry powder	7 mL
¼ cup	water	50 mL
1 tsp.	salt	5 mL
2	hard-cooked eggs, finely chopped	2
⅓ cup	minced fresh parsley	75 mL
1-2	jalepēno or green chili peppers, chopped (depending on your firefighting ability — use 1 or 2 peppers)	1-2
½ cup	vegetable oil	125 mL

- Heat 3 tbsp. (45 mL) oil in heavy skillet over medium heat. Add ginger and garlic and stir for 1 minute. Add cumin and curry powder.
- Add beef and brown gently. Mix in water and salt and cook approximately 5 minutes until liquid evaporates but meat is still moist, stirring frequently.

- Cool completely. Stir in eggs, parsley and chilies.
- Divide dough into 8 balls. Working with 1 piece at a time (cover remainder) roll dough ball on lightly floured surface into a 10" (25 cm) circle.
- Spread ⅓ cup (75 mL) stuffing in center of dough. Brush borders with water and fold sides in; press to seal and completely enclose filling. Set aside and cover with plastic. Repeat with remaining dough; do not let breads touch.
- In a heavy skillet over medium heat, cook bread in batches until spotted brown, about 1 minute per side. Drizzle 1 tbsp. (15 mL) oil over and around each bread. Continue cooking until golden brown and crisp, turning occasionally, about 2 minutes. Wipe skillet clean between batches.
- Transfer to plate and keep warm. Mogul bread is an excellent appetizer or, along with another dish, would provide a luncheon that would certainly see you through to the end of the day. Sour cream or yogurt are superb condiments to serve with this recipe.
- Serves 3-4.

BEEF 'N' PITA POCKET

Looking for something different, something totally different? Don't pass up this beef offering, tucked away so tastily in a pita pocket!

12 oz.	*lean ground beef	340 g
1 tbsp.	minced fresh parsley	15 mL
1	garlic clove, minced	1
½ tsp.	salt	2 mL
dash	freshly ground pepper	dash
dash	oregano leaves	dash
2 tsp.	olive oil	10 mL
½ cup	sliced onions	125 mL
1	medium red bell pepper, roasted, peeled, seeded, cut into strips **	1
¼ cup	finely chopped celery	50 mL
1	medium tomato, chopped	1
2 pieces	pita bread, heated	2 pieces

- Combine beef, parsley, garlic, salt, pepper and oregano. Form mixture into 4 wiener shapes approximately 2" (5 cm) long. Broil beef rolls in oven until evenly browned on all sides. Keep warm.
- Heat oil in skillet, sauté onion until soft. Add pepper strips, celery and tomato; sauté 1 minute longer.
- Cut the pita bread in half, opening to form a 'pocket.' Stuff each pocket with half of the vegetable mixture and a beef roll. Top with mustard.
- Serves 2.

**To roast pepper, place on broiler pan and broil approximately 6" (15 cm) from heat, turning to char on all sides.

THREE-ALARM CHILI CON CARNE

Chili can be served almost anywhere, anytime and to anyone, providing they have lived through their first encounter with chili. This volatile beef dish is sneaky and without your being aware, it can creep up on you!

A robust, young, California Zinfandel is a must, along with garlic or cheese bread, and a humongous salad, topped with hundreds and hundreds of crispy, toasted garlic croutons.

2 lbs.	*lean ground beef	1 kg
2 x 19 oz.	can red kidney beans	2 x 540 mL
2	garlic cloves, minced	2
1	green pepper, cored, finely chopped	1
1	medium onion, chopped	1
4 slices	bacon, cooked, cut into ½" (1.5 cm) pieces	4 slices
4 tsp.	chili powder	20 mL
2 tsp.	salt	10 mL
¼ tsp.	freshly ground pepper	1 mL
¼-½ tsp.	cayenne pepper	1-2 mL
½ tsp.	dried oregano	2 mL
1	bay leaf	1
3 drops	Tabasco	3 drops
½ cup	ketchup	125 mL
½ cup	tomato paste	125 mL
3½ cups	peeled and chopped tomatoes	875 mL
OR		
28 oz.	can tomatoes	796 mL

- Place the kidney beans in a sieve and rinse thoroughly with cold water.
- In a very large saucepan or Dutch oven, sauté beef with garlic until golden brown. Add green pepper and onion; sauté for 3 minutes. Reduce heat to medium. Add kidney beans, cooked bacon and all remaining ingredients. Stir constantly until bubbly.
- Quickly reduce heat, cover loosely with foil and simmer chili 4 to 6 hours.
- Chili should not contain too much liquid. If chili becomes runny, remove foil covering during last couple of hours.
- Serves 6-8.

La Salsa Perfetta (The Perfect Sauce), page 99

KIMA

An unusual name, but then this is an unusual, but o-o-o-oh so-o-o good beef dish! Peanuts, bananas and coconut juice served with beef? You bet, and while you might not wish to serve KIMA every week . . . your family will, undoubtedly, ask for that dinner with the funny name every so often.

1 lb.	*lean ground beef	500 kg
2 tbsp.	vegetable oil	30 mL
1	small onion, finely chopped	1
½	red pepper, finely chopped	½
½	green pepper, finely chopped	½
½ lb.	fresh tomatoes cut in sections	250 g
½ cup	ground peanuts	125 mL
1 cup	mashed bananas	250 mL
dash	salt	dash
1½ tsp.	curry powder	7 mL
4 cups	cooked rice, cooked in coconut juice	1 L

- In large skillet, heat oil, add beef and cook thoroughly. Remove any excess oil.
- Add onion, red pepper, green pepper and tomatoes. Cook until tender. Add peanuts and banana. Add salt and curry and simmer for 1 hour over medium heat.
- Serve with rice cooked in coconut juice. Fresh sesame bread sticks, a zappy green salad and a vegetable side dish will surely help your family remember Kima.
- Serves 4-6.

FRANK AND BURGER LOAF

Nothing is more satisfying on a blustery winter day than to stock the fireplace with kindling and logs in preparation for a warm, cozy dinner-setting of Alberta Baked Beans, page 162, and a Frank and Burger Loaf.

Throw-pillows, paper plates, brightly colored serviettes, lemonade, yes, even lemonade, all served on a tablecloth spread in front of a warm, cozy fire. Your heart will be warmed by the fun and flow of conversation from every member of your family as they shut out white snow and winter winds!

1 lb.	*lean ground beef	500 g
1	round loaf Italian bread	1
½ cup	evaporated milk	125 mL
1	egg	1
1 tbsp.	minced onion	15 mL
2 tbsp.	chopped green pepper	30 mL
1 tbsp.	chopped pimiento	15 mL
1 tsp.	salt	5 mL
dash	freshly ground pepper	dash
dash	celery salt	dash
2	frankfurters	2
4-5	sweet gherkins	4-5

- Cut thin slice from top of bread, much like cutting the lid off a pumpkin. Carefully scoop out enough crumbs from center to make 2 cups (500 mL), loosely packed. Set bread shell and top aside. Preheat oven to 375°F (190°C).
- Combine in a large bowl, crumbs, milk and egg; let stand for 10 minutes. Mix beef, onion, green pepper, pimiento, salt, pepper and celery salt thoroughly.
- Spread half of meat mixture evenly on bottom of bread shell. Cut 2 wieners crosswise into 3 equal sections and place end to end on top of meat mixture in a circle in shell. Place 4 or 5 gherkins, laid end to end, in a smaller circle on the inside of the wieners.
- Top with rest of meat mixture, filling shell. Replace bread top, secure with toothpicks. Place on cookie sheet, cover loosely with foil. Bake 1½ hours.
- To serve, remove toothpicks and cut into wedges.
- Serves 6 comfortably.

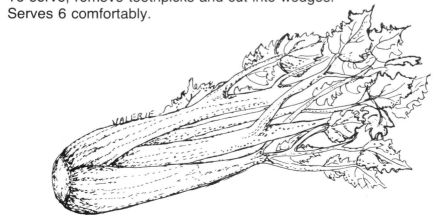

TAMALE PIE

Cool down your hot tamale pie with a scrumptious Caesar salad, page 150, a dip and a dish of crunchy fresh vegetables.

1 lb.	*lean ground beef	500 g
1	medium onion, chopped	1
2 stalks	celery, chopped	2 stalks
1	green pepper, chopped	1
14 oz.	can tomato sauce	398 mL
1 tbsp.	chili powder	15 mL
2 drops	Tabasco sauce	2 drops
1 tsp.	salt	5 mL
3 tbsp.	corn relish	45 mL
3 tbsp.	thinly sliced olives	45 mL

CORNMEAL COVER

¾ cup	yellow cornmeal	175 mL
dash	salt	dash
2 cups	cold water	500 mL
1 tbsp.	butter	15 mL
¼ cup	grated Cheddar cheese	50 mL
2 cups	cold water	500 mL

TAMALE TOPPER

2 tbsp.	cold water	30 mL
2 tsp.	cornstarch	10 mL
1 cup	tomatoes canned, cut up	250 mL
2 tbsp.	seeded, chopped, canned green chili peppers	30 mL
2 tbsp.	chopped green pepper	30 mL
1 tsp.	Worcestershire sauce	5 mL

Tamale Topper

- Sauté ground beef. Add onion, celery and green pepper. Cook about 3 minutes. Remove any excess fat. Add tomato sauce, chili powder, Tabasco and salt. Simmer for about 20 minutes or until mixture is thick. Add corn relish and olives. Pour into greased 9" x 2" (2 L) round pan.
- For the CORNMEAL COVER, stir cornmeal and salt into cold water in saucepan. Cook, stirring constantly, until thick. Add butter and cheese and mix well. Spread evenly over hot meat mixture. Bake at 400°F (200°C) for 40 minutes, or until topping is golden brown.
- For the TAMALE TOPPER, blend cold water with cornstarch in small saucepan. Stir in undrained tomatoes, chili peppers, green pepper and Worcestershire sauce. Cook and stir until thickened and bubbly. Serve warm over individual servings of tamale pie!
- Serves 4-6.

EMPANADAS

The most incredible, spicy, moist, mouth-watering meat turnovers you will ever taste! Absolutely delicious hot or cold. A most welcome treat for the lunch-bunch school kids. Be prepared to serve several at any one time 'cause one or two just aren't enough! Empanadas are also great served hot as an appetizer.

PASTRY

2 cups	all-purpose flour	500 mL
½ tsp.	salt	2 mL
¼ tsp.	cayenne pepper	1 mL
⅔ cup	butter	150 mL
¼ cup	ice water	50 mL

FILLING

1 tbsp.	butter	15 mL
1	garlic clove, minced	1
1	small onion, finely chopped	1
1 lb.	*lean ground beef	500 g
2	tomatoes, peeled and chopped	2
1 tsp.	curry powder	5 mL
2 tbsp.	ketchup	30 mL
dash	salt	dash
dash	pepper	dash
2 tbsp.	all-purpose flour	30 mL
¼ cup	beef bouillon (page 148)	50 mL

GLAZE

1	egg	1
2 tsp.	water	10 mL

- Sift flour, salt and cayenne together into mixing bowl. Using a pastry blender, cut in butter until mixture resembles peas. Gradually add enough water to form ball of dough. Refrigerate for at least 30 minutes while preparing filling.
- In a large frying pan melt butter over medium heat; cook garlic and onion until tender. Add beef and cook until lightly browned. Stir frequently. Add tomatoes, curry, ketchup, salt and pepper to taste. Stir well.
- Gently sprinkle flour over mixture, stirring constantly to blend. Pour in beef bouillon and cook, stirring constantly until mixture thickens. Reduce heat and simmer, covered for 10 minutes.
- Remove from heat and refrigerate until cool before assembling.
- Vigorously beat egg and water until mixed thoroughly.
- On lightly floured surface, roll out half the pastry ⅛" (3 mm) thick and cut out 5" (12 cm) circles. Spoon 2 tbsp. (30mL) of the filling onto center of each pastry circle.

- Brush edges of pastry with glaze. Fold circle in half over the filling. Pinch with fingers to seal the seam. Brush tops of turnovers with glaze. Pierce the pastry with a fork to allow steam to escape.
- Bake at 400°F (200°C) for 25 minutes or until golden brown.
- Makes 12 to 14 empanadas.

QUICK PIROSHKI

Everyone from time to time needs more time.Quick Piroshki offers the time needed to catch up or, better still, time to get ahead. If you can get ahead of the crowd, you are deemed, leader of the parade.

And no one will dare rain on your parade of culinary treats as you serve Piroshki, fresh green peas, creamed cauliflower, celery sticks, vinegar-marinated cucumbers and warmed cheese bread. Oh! please, may we come for dinner? You can find us in the southwest corner of Alberta . . . listed under hungry!

12 oz.	*lean ground beef	340 g
1	pie crust packaged mix	1
2	large onions minced	2
2 tbsp.	butter	30 mL
2	hard-cooked eggs, chopped	2
1 tsp.	dried dill	5 mL
1 tsp.	dried chives	5 mL
¾ tsp.	salt	3 mL
⅛ tsp.	freshly ground pepper	0.5 mL
⅓ cup	Cheddar cheese old, grated	75 mL
1	egg, lightly beaten, for glaze	1

- Preheat oven to 400°F (200°C). Prepare pie crust mixture according to instructions. Roll out and cut into 2'' (5 cm) circles.
- Sauté onions in butter until golden. Add meat and cook, stirring until light brown. Cool mixture and add all remaining ingredients. Mix thoroughly.
- Place 1 tsp. (5 mL) in center of each circle. Fold pastry over filling, crimp and seal edges with fingers.
- Place on greased cookie sheet, make small slash to allow steam to escape and brush with beaten egg. Bake for 30 minutes or until golden brown.
- Serve immediately.
- Serves 6.

PINWHEELS à la BEEF

A long-time, in fact, childhood favorite. The visual presentation of beef pinwheels is very attractive and immediately the old taste buds start to work. They will keep on working as you enjoy the satisfying taste and surprise garnish for this beef dish.

1 lb.	*lean ground beef	500 g
1 tbsp.	vegetable oil	15 mL
1 cup	finely chopped onion	250 mL
¼ cup	ketchup	50 mL
¼ tsp.	pepper	1 mL
¾ cup	cream of celery soup	175 mL
2 cups	all-purpose flour	500 mL
¾ cup	yellow cornmeal	175 mL
2 tbsp.	baking powder	30 mL
½ tsp.	cayenne	2 mL
½ tsp.	salt	2 mL
2 tsp.	dry mustard	10 mL
⅓ cup	butter	75 mL
¾ cup	milk	175 mL

- In skillet heat oil and sauté beef and onion. Remove to a bowl, stir in ketchup, pepper and soup. Cool.
- Combine flour, cornmeal, baking powder, cayenne and salt. Cut in butter until mixture resembles peas.
- Stir in milk. Dough should be stiff. On a floured board, knead mixture 10-12 times. Roll out to form a 12" (30 cm) square.
- Add water to dry mustard to form a medium paste. Spread lightly over the surface of dough. Cover with meat and roll up as in a jelly roll. Pinch seam together. Cut into 6 slices. Place in greased pan and bake at 400°F (200°C) oven for 20-25 minutes.
- Surprise sauce!!! Gently warm cranberry sauce in a double boiler. Serve in side dish, make sure you have lots because you will be surprised at the number of requests for seconds.
- Serves 4-6.

COUNTRY PIE

Do you remember the expression, 'don't judge a book by its cover'? Well, this little recipe would surely fit into that category . . . simple to make, inexpensive to prepare and for all those little cattle rustlers, superb!

Add a cosmopolitan touch by serving a Green Goddess Salad, page 155, along with a vegetable side dish and you will probably be elevated to the status of the 'Supreme One' for the day. Play your cards right, serve another delicious beef recipe tomorrow evening and you just might maintain that handle for a protracted period of time.

1 lb.	*lean ground beef	500 g
½ cup	dry bread crumbs	125 mL
¼ cup	chopped onion	50 mL
¼ cup	chopped green pepper	50 mL
1 tsp.	salt	5 mL
¼ tsp.	pepper	1 mL
dash	celery salt	dash
2 x 7½ oz.	can tomato sauce	2 x 213 g
3 cups	cooked rice	750 mL
½ cup	processed cheese	125 mL

- Mix beef, bread crumbs, onion, green pepper, seasonings and ½ can of tomato sauce. Spread in a greased 9" x 2" (22 x 5 cm) pie pan, forming a shell.
- Mix rice, cheese and remaining tomato sauce. Place in meat shell. Sprinkle top with a little additional cheese.
- Bake in moderate oven 350°F (180°C) 35-40 minutes until meat is done. Cut into wedge-shaped pieces.
- Serves 6.

BEEF TOURTIÈRE

A wonderful, 1-dish meal just right for one of those many blustery, Canadian winter days that somehow we manage to survive.

Interesting — some survive, whilst others thrive. Think of all the children, rosy-cheeked and wet-kneed, home from the toboggan hill, needing something filling and warm. Ah, Tourtière waiting!

And skiers, 12 runs later on good packed snow with light snow falling all day. Tourtière . . . and a bottle of LOIRE. What a spectacular finish to a weekend.

CHEDDAR CRUST

1½ cups	all-purpose flour	375 mL
⅓ cup	grated, old, Cheddar cheese	75 mL
½ tsp.	salt	2 mL
¼ cup	unsalted butter, chilled, cut into pieces	50 mL
¼ cup	shortening	50 mL
¼ cup	ice water	50 mL

FILLING

3 tbsp.	vegetable oil	45 mL
2	medium onions, minced	2
2	medium garlic cloves, minced	2
1 lb.	*lean ground beef	500 g
½ lb.	ground pork	250 g
2	medium tomatoes, peeled, and finely chopped	2
¼ cup	water	50 mL
½ tsp.	cinnamon	2 mL
½ tsp.	allspice	2 mL
½ tsp.	dried savory, crumbled	2 mL
¼ tsp.	celery salt	1 mL
dash	ground cloves	dash
½ cup	fresh breadcrumbs	125 mL
dash	salt	dash
dash	pepper	dash
1 tbsp.	Dijon-style mustard	15 mL

GLAZE

1	egg, beaten with	1
2 tbsp.	whipping cream	30 mL

BEEF TOURTIÈRE (CONT'D.)

- In a large bowl combine flour, cheese and salt. Cut in butter and shortening until mixture resembles peas. Blend in ice water so that dough holds together. Add more water if necessary. Divide dough in half. Shape into balls. Wrap in plastic. Chill while preparing filling.
- In large skillet heat oil over medium-low heat. Add onions and garlic. Cover and cook until translucent, about 10 minutes, stirring occasionally. Add beef and pork. Cook until no longer pink.
- Add tomatoes, water, cinnamon, allspice, savory, celery salt and cloves. Reduce heat to medium-low and simmer until most of the liquid is absorbed, about 30 minutes. Stir in bread crumbs, salt and pepper. Cool.
- Roll 1 portion of dough out on lightly floured board into a ⅛" (½ cm) thick circle. Roll dough round rolling pin and unroll into a 9" x 2" (22 x 5 cm) deep-dish pie pan.
- Brush bottom with mustard. Spoon filling into crust. Roll remaining dough out on lightly floured board into a ⅛" (½ cm) thick circle. Drape pastry over dish, crimping edges to seal, trim excess. Be creative and reroll scraps of dough and cut out patterns to place on top of pastry.
- Score the top of crust to allow steam to escape. Brush with glaze. (This can be prepared 1 day ahead . . . just cover and refrigerate).
- Preheat oven to 425°F (220°C). Bake pie 10 minutes. Reduce oven temperature to 350°F (180°C) and continue baking until golden brown, about 35 minutes. If top browns too quickly loosely drape with foil.
- Serves 6-8 hungry skiers.

BEEF QUICHE INCREDIBLE

Easy elegance, Beef Quiche Incredible makes its own crust!

1 lb.	*lean ground beef	500 g
1	onion, sliced	1
1	green pepper, finely chopped	1
¼ cup	chopped green olives	50 mL
1 stalk	celery, finely chopped	1 stalk
3 tbsp.	finely chopped, red pepper	45 mL
½ tsp.	salt	2 mL
¼ tsp.	pepper	1 mL
1 cup	grated Swiss cheese	250 mL
1½ cups	milk	375 mL
¾ cup	tea biscuit mix	175 mL
3	eggs	3

- Grease a 9" x 2" (2.5 L) round pan. Sauté ground beef. Add onion and green pepper, cook until tender. Drain any excess fat.
- Quickly stir in olives, celery, red pepper, salt and pepper. Spread meat and vegetable mixture in pan. Sprinkle with cheese.
- Beat milk, biscuit mix and eggs until smooth, 15 seconds in blender on high or 1 minute with hand beater. Pour over beef and vegetables.
- Bake at 400°F (200°C) for 40-45 minutes or until knife inserted in centre comes out clean. Cool 5 minutes before serving.
- Serves 6-8 . . . all of whom will be wearing a 'happy face' when they have finished sampling Beef Quiche Incredible. A green salad with a bouncy oil and vinegar dressing will provide a nice balance to this beef dish.
- Quiche, coffee and companionship . . . a perfect finish for a busy day!

ECONOMY
WITH FLAIR AND FLAVOR

- BEEF RIBS

- STEWS

- SOUPS

- VARIETY CUTS

OVEN-BARBECUED SHORT RIBS
WITH CHILI BISCUITS

Enormous self-satisfaction prevails when you can provide a scrumptious dinner for either your family or your guests at a very reasonable cost.

Short ribs and Chili Biscuits offers this and more, TASTE, especially taste, with chili powder, cheese, Tabasco and time for mellowing-out.

So be a friend and share. Be a special friend and share Oven-Barbecued Short Ribs with Chili Biscuits!

3 lbs.	*beef short ribs, cut into 1" (2.5 cm) pieces	1.4 kg
3 tbsp.	vegetable oil	45 mL
2	onions, coarsely chopped	2
4	large garlic cloves, minced	4
19 oz.	can tomatoes, undrained	540 mL
2 cups	beef bouillon (page 148)	500 g
⅓ cup	cider vinegar	75 mL
¼ cup	firmly packed brown sugar	50 mL
4 tbsp.	Worcestershire sauce	60 mL
2 tbsp.	Dijon-style mustard	30 mL
2 drops	Tabasco	2 drops
1½ tsp.	salt	7 mL
1½ tsp.	cayenne pepper	7 mL
½ tsp.	freshly ground pepper	2 mL
½ tsp.	paprika	2 mL
½ tsp.	ground turmeric	2 mL
10 sprigs	parsley, tied	10 sprigs
2	lemon slices ¼" (1 cm)	2
1 lb.	potatoes, cut in 1" (2.5 cm) cubes	500 g
1 lb.	carrots, cut in 1" (2.5 cm) cubes	500 g

- Preheat broiler. Arrange ribs in single layer in large shallow roasting pan. Broil approximately 4" (10 cm) from heat until brown, turning frequently, about 10 minutes.

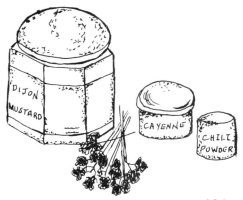

OVEN-BARBECUED SHORT RIBS
WITH CHILI BISCUITS (CONT'D.)

- Preheat oven to 350°F (180°C). Heat oil in Dutch oven over medium-low heat. Add onions, garlic, celery and cook until soft and golden brown, stirring frequently, about 10 minutes. Add ribs and any drippings. Stir in tomatoes, broth, vinegar, sugar, Worcestershire sauce, mustard, Tabasco, salt, cayenne, pepper, paprika, turmeric, parsley and lemon. Increase heat and bring to boil.
- Place in oven, cover and bake until short ribs are tender, about 2 hours.
- Stir potatoes and carrots into ribs. Cover and bake until vegetables are tender, about 40 minutes. During last 10 minutes remove cover to reduce the amount of sauce.
- Increase oven temperature to 450°F (230°C). Arrange chili biscuits (below) over ribs. Bake uncovered until biscuits are puffed and lightly browned, about 15 minutes.
- Serve immediately for 6-8 lucky people

CHILI BISCUITS

1 tbsp.	unsalted butter	15 mL
1	medium onion	1
1	garlic clove, minced	1
2 cups	sifted all-purpose flour	500 mL
1 tbsp.	baking powder	15 mL
2 tsp.	chili powder	10 mL
½ tsp.	cayenne pepper	2 mL
1 tsp.	salt	5 mL
¼ cup	grated Parmesan cheese	50 mL
2 tbsp.	minced fresh parsley	30 mL
⅓ cup	solid vegetable shortening	75 mL
¾ cup	milk	175 mL

- Melt butter in small, heavy saucepan over medium heat. Add onion and garlic and cook until soft, stirring occasionally, about 10 minutes. Cool mixture 10 minutes.
- Stir flour, baking powder, chili powder, cayenne pepper and salt in large bowl. Stir in cheese and parsley. Cut in shortening with pastry blender until mixture resembles peas. Blend in onion mixture. Form a well in center of flour mixture. Add milk to well and mix with fork just until dough comes together. Turn dough out onto lightly floured surface and knead 3 to 5 times. Roll dough out to ½" (1 cm) thickness. Cut out biscuits using 3" (7½ cm) floured cutter.

SIZZLING SPICED SHORT RIBS

Short ribs smothered in a mean and lean barbecue sauce, then gently braised for 2 hours, French bread spread with garlic butter and slowly oven-warmed along with a pizazzzy salad, constitute the perfect dinner.

Friends, you never knew you had so many, and most of them wanting to visit you just about Spicy Short Rib time.

4 lbs.	*beef short ribs, boneless, if available	2 kg
2 tbsp.	vegetable oil	30 mL
2	onions, sliced	2
2 tbsp.	dry mustard	30 mL
2 tbsp.	Worcestershire sauce	30 mL
2 drops	Tabasco sauce	2 drops
1 tsp.	salt	5 mL
2 tsp.	curry powder	10 mL
½ tsp.	cayenne pepper	2 mL
2 tbsp.	ketchup	30 mL
¼ cup	red wine	50 mL
⅔ cup	water	150 mL

- In a large heavy casserole, heat oil over medium heat and brown short ribs. Remove excess fat. Stir in onions and set aside.
- In a small bowl, mix together mustard, Worcestershire, Tabasco sauce, salt, curry powder, cayenne, ketchup, wine and water. Pour over beef.
- Cook, covered in a 350°F (180°C) oven for 2 hours or until tender.
- Serves 4-6.

BEEF BONES

Beef bones — an excellent serving for weekend gatherings. They are inexpensive and can be made well in advance.

Beef bones are also super when, with a huge serviette tucked under one's chin, everyone in the family can dig in 'à la caveman'. Beef bones taste superb with fresh corn on the cob, warm, crusty garlic toast and a whopping Caesar salad, page 150.

	*lean beef ribs, enough for your family	
⅔ cup	prepared spicy brown mustard	150 mL
1 tbsp.	firmly packed brown sugar	15 mL
⅔ cup	bread crumbs	150 mL
dash	freshly ground pepper	dash

BEEF BONES (CONT'D.)

- Will provide glaze for 2 racks of beef ribs which will serve 6.
- Preheat oven to 450°F (230°C). Cut ribs into individual beef sticks. Combine mustard and sugar. Using a brush, generously coat each rib with mixture. Roll in bread crumbs and pepper to coat thoroughly.
- Arrange ribs rounded side up on a broiler pan and bake 30-40 minutes, or until ribs are nicely browned and excess fat has dripped off. Serve immediately.
- Serves 6.

MUAU LUAU SHORT RIBS

4 lbs.	*beef short ribs, in serving-size pieces	2 kg
19 oz.	can pineapple slices	540 mL
¼ cup	water	50 mL
¼ cup	soy sauce	50 mL
1 tsp.	ground ginger	5 mL
2 tbsp.	finely grated orange rind	30 mL
	juice from 1 orange	
1 tbsp.	brown sugar	15 mL
¼ cup	honey	50 mL
1 tbsp.	cornstarch	15 mL
¼ cup	water	50 mL

- Pierce short ribs several times with a meat fork. Place in a deep bowl. Combine juice from pineapple with ¼ cup (50 mL) water, soy sauce, ginger, sugar and honey. Pour over ribs. Cover and marinate in the refrigerator for 24 hours, turning occasionally. Drain, reserving marinade.
- Broil or barbecue ribs for 15-20 minutes or until cooked. Brush with reserved marinade during latter part of cooking.
- A few minutes before meat is cooked, brush pineapple slices with marinade and barbecue or broil until golden.
- To thicken marinade for sauce, combine 1 tbsp. (15 mL) cornstarch with ¼ cup (50 mL) cold water. Stir into marinade and heat until sauce thickens and becomes clear. Serve sauce with ribs and pineapple.
- Serves 6.

ginger

GRILLED CRANBERRY & PINEAPPLE SHORT RIBS

Perfect for company! Beef short ribs, leisurely simmered, bring to the table the most savory, tender, tasty and economical beef serving you can imagine.

Garlic croûtons sitting as 'kings of the castle' atop a freshly turned out salad and a green vegetable side dish will, without reservation, please even the most discriminating family member, including even our delightful, sensitive and outgoing teen-age sons.

6 lbs.	beef short ribs, in serving-sized pieces	3 kg
2 tsp.	salt	10 mL
dash	pepper	dash
½ cup	water	125 mL
2 x 13 oz.	jars pineapple preserve	2 x 375 mL
1 cup	whole cranberry sauce	250 mL
2 tbsp.	marmalade	30 mL
1 cup	chili sauce	250 mL
½ cup	vinegar	125 mL

- Trim excess fat from ribs and sprinkle with salt and pepper.
- Place ribs in a Dutch oven and add water. Cover and simmer for approximately 2 hours, or until meat is tender. If necessary during cooking, add water.
- Drain ribs. Combine preserve, cranberry sauce, marmalade, chili sauce and vinegar. Brush some of the glaze mixture over the ribs. Broil ribs in oven, on second lowest rack from bottom. Brush ribs with glaze and turn frequently for 15 to 20 minutes. (Also great on the barbecue . . . cook over slow coals for approximately same time).
- Heat remaining glaze and pass with the best ribs you've tasted since the last time you cooked Grilled Cranberry & Pineapple Ribs.
- Serves 6.
- See photograph opposite.

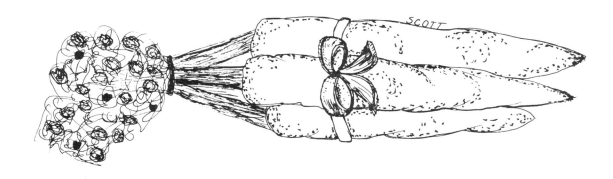

Grilled Cranberry & Pineapple Short Ribs, page 128
Eggs à la Neige, page 165

MOSTACCIOLI BEEF STEW

PASTA, a contemporary food for the 80's, Mostaccioli and beef, hey, what a treat!

Mostaccioli is a large macaroni whose ends are always cut diagonally. Should you have any leftovers . . . this recipe is great for tomorrow's lunch thermos.

1½ lb.	*lean beef, inside or outside round cut in 1" (2.5 cm) cubes	750 g
2 tbsp.	vegetable oil	30 mL
½	onion, chopped	½
1	garlic clove, pressed	1
1 stalk	celery, thinly sliced	1 stalk
¼ cup	water	50 mL
2	bay leaves	2
3 cups	beef bouillon (page 148)	750 mL
7½ oz.	can tomato sauce	213 mL
2 tbsp.	butter	30 mL
1½ tsp.	salt	7 mL
½ tsp.	freshly ground pepper	2 mL
½ tsp.	oregano	2 mL
3 cups	uncooked mostaccioli	750 mL
10 oz.	frozen peas, thawed (or other vegetable)	285 g

- Heat oil in a heavy 5-quart (5 L) pot. Add meat, onion, garlic, celery, water and bay leaves. Cover and simmer 1 hour over low heat.
- Add beef bouillon, tomato sauce, butter, salt, pepper and oregano. Bring to a boil. Add mostaccioli and bring to a boil again, stirring constantly. Cover and cook 10 minutes.
- Uncover, stir in peas. Cook 5 minutes longer until mostaccioli is done.
- Remove bay leaves. Top with grated Parmesan cheese. Serve immediately.
- Serves 6.

*LEAN BEEF — AN IMPORTANT SOURCE OF IRON!

The iron found in beef is in a form that is much more readily absorbed by the body than the iron in vegetables and cereals. For example, your body absorbs as much iron from 90 g (3 oz.) of beef as from a 228 g (8 oz.) of spinach.

And the good news continues . . . including meat in your regular diet increases the absorption of iron from other food sources.

CHINESE WONTON BEEF STEW

In the mood for something new? Do you enjoy a taste that is just a little different? Then stop right here! . . . Chinese Wonton Beef Stew, traditional and, at the same time, very much a part of today's mainstream.

1½ lbs.	*lean beef stew meat, cut in 1" (2.5 cm) cubes	750 g
2 slices	bacon, finely chopped	2 slices
1	medium onion, chopped	1
1	garlic clove, minced	1
1 stalk	celery, finely chopped	1 stalk
2 tbsp.	vegetable oil	30 mL
½ cup	dry white wine	125 mL
¼ cup	soy sauce	50 mL
2 tsp.	beef bouillon granules	10 mL
2 tsp.	sugar	10 mL
½ tsp.	ground ginger	2 mL
3¾ cups	water, divided	925 mL
½ tsp.	pepper, freshly ground	2 mL
3 cups	coarsely chopped bok choy	750 mL
1 cup	sliced, fresh mushrooms	250 mL
6 oz.	frozen pea pods	170 g
¼ cup	cornstarch	50 mL
20	Wontons (see opposite)	20

- Cook meat, bacon, onion, celery and garlic in oil in a 4-quart (4 L) Dutch oven until meat is browned.
- Add wine, soy, bouillon granules, sugar, ginger, pepper and 875 mL (3½ cups) water. Bring to a boil, reduce heat. Cover and simmer 1½ hours or until meat is tender, stir occasionally.
- Add bok choy, mushrooms and pea pods to stew. Simmer for 2 or 3 minutes. Blend cornstarch and ¼ cup (50 mL) cold water; stir into hot mixture. Cook and stir until thickened and bubbly. Add hot wontons.
- Serves 4-6.

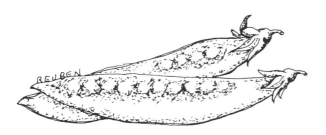

WONTONS

4 oz.	canned shrimp	113 g
1	egg yolk, beaten	1
½ cup	finely chopped bok choy	125 mL
¼ cup	finely chopped onion	50 mL
1 tbsp.	soy sauce	15 mL
½ tsp.	sugar	2 mL
¼ tsp.	ground ginger	1 mL
½ tsp.	salt	2 mL
dash	pepper, freshly ground	dash
20	wonton skins	20

● Drain and chop shrimp. Combine shrimp, egg yolk, bok choy, onion, soy sauce, sugar, ginger, salt and pepper.

WRAPPING WONTONS

● Buy wonton skins at the supermarket. If wonton skins are not available, egg roll skins cut in quarters may be substituted.
● Position squared wonton skin with 1 point toward you. Place 1 tbsp. (15 mL) of filling just off the center of skin.
● Fold point closest to you over and slightly under the filling. Complete the roll to the top of the skin.
● Moisten right-hand corner of skin with water.
● Grasp right and left-hand corners bringing these corners together underneath the filling.
● Overlap left-hand corner over right-hand corner, press to seal.
● In a large saucepan cover and cook wontons in boiling water for 3 to 5 mintues. Drain. Add to stew.

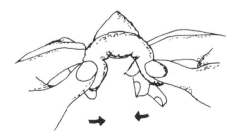

ESTOFADO CON CIRUELAS Y PINONES

BEEF STEW WITH PRUNES AND PINE NUTS

Estupendo estofado!! A Spanish exclamation for a beef stew that, while somewhat commonplace in Spain, is quite unknown on this continent. This surely is an example of those times when, if you don't identify the ingredients of a serving, your eating public will undoubtedly enjoy, enjoy and enjoy.

2 lbs.	*lean beef stew meats in 2" (5 cm) cubes	1 kg
⅓-½ cup	olive oil	75-125 mL
1	medium onion, thickly sliced	1
2	garlic cloves, minced	2
1½	large tomatoes, unpeeled, cut into 8 pieces	1½
3 tbsp.	cognac	45 mL
½ cup	dry white wine	125 mL
to taste	salt	to taste
½ tsp.	paprika	2 mL
⅛ tsp.	cinnamon	0.5 mL
1 sprig	fresh thyme OR	1 sprig
½ tsp.	dried thyme	2 mL
½	bay leaf	½
1½ tbsp.	flour	22 mL
1 cup	boiling water	250 mL
½ lb.	dried prunes	250 g
½ cup	pine nuts	125 mL

- In large, heavy skillet heat 3 tbsp. (45 mL) olive oil. When oil is just about to start smoking, brown the meat rapidly in small batches. As the meat browns, transfer to bowl.
- Add olive oil if needed to brown the onion and garlic. Add tomato and fry until the juice has evaporated. Add cognac and wine and cook over high heat until the liquid evaporates. Reduce the heat; add the salt, paprika, cinnamon, thyme, bay leaf and flour. Stir until the flour is browned. Return the meat to the skillet. Add boiling water, cover and simmer until the meat is tender — about 2 hours.
- If the sauce becomes too dry during cooking, add boiling water in small amounts. If the sauce is too thin when meat is done, remove the meat and boil the sauce, uncovered, until thick enough.
- 15 minutes before serving, boil the pine nuts in water to cover. Drain and add the pine nuts and prunes to the estofado.
- Prunes are added at the last moment to avoid oversweetening the sauce and pine nuts are added just before serving to preserve their whiteness.
- Estofado is 'hostess friendly". This beef dish is even better if prepared several hours in advance and reheated just before serving.
- Serves 4.

BOEUF BOURGUIGNON

A wonderful beef dish, flavored with a bouquet garni, steeped in red wine and Madeira with a splash of brandy. Definitely company fare when served with buttered flat noodles, asparagus tips, garlic bread and dessert!

4 lbs.	*lean chuck beef, cut in 1½" (4 cm) cubes	2 kg
¼ cup	butter, divided	50 mL
3 tbsp.	flour	45 mL
dash	salt	dash
dash	pepper	dash
1½ cup	red wine	375 mL
2	onions, coarsely chopped	2
2	shallots, finely chopped	2
1	carrot, cut up	1
1	garlic clove, finely chopped	1
1	bouquet garni	1
1	veal knuckle, cracked	1
	water	
1 lb.	mushroom caps	500 g
¼ cup	Madeira wine	50 mL
2 tbsp.	brandy	30 mL

- In large skillet sauté beef in 3 tbsp. (45 mL) butter until evenly browned. Remove any excess fat.
- Sprinkle meat with flour, blend in thoroughly and add salt, pepper and red wine.
- Brown onions in 1 tbsp. (15 mL) butter in a small skillet. Add onions to meat and stir.
- Add shallots, carrot, garlic, bouquet garni and veal knuckle. Add just enough water to cover meat. Cover and simmer for 2 hours over low heat or until meat is very tender.
- Half an hour before serving, add mushroom caps, Madeira and brandy. Remove bouquet garni and veal bone.
- Taste and adjust seasoning and thicken slightly with a flour-water mixture if necessary.
- A Burgundy such as Mâcon Rouge might really be appreciated by any of those lucky 6 or 8 diners gracing your table.

DIJON AND COGNAC BEEF STEW

This full-flavored dish needs only a simple green salad, warm, whole-wheat dinner rolls and a vegetable side dish to make everyone around your dinner table sit back, content and comfortable.

This delectable beef serving is even better the second day. Dijon and Cognac beef stew is a great 'freezer friendly' recipe.

2 lbs.	*lean beef chuck, trimmed and cut into 1" (2.5 cm) cubes	1 kg
4 oz.	salt pork, blanched 5 minutes (rind removed and reserved), cut into small cubes	125 g
1	large onion, chopped	1
3	large shallots, chopped	3
	flour	
	butter	
¼ cup	good quality cognac	50 mL
2 cups	beef bouillon (page 148)	500 mL
1 tbsp.	Dijon-style mustard	15 mL
1 tbsp.	coarse-ground French mustard	15 mL
3	large carrots, cut bite-size	3
dash	salt	dash
dash	freshly ground pepper	dash
dash	garlic salt	dash
2 tbsp.	butter	30 mL
7 oz.	fresh, small mushrooms, halved	200 g
dash	freshly ground pepper	dash
¼ cup	full-bodied red wine	50 mL
1 tbsp.	coarse-ground French mustard	15 mL

- Cook salt pork in heavy skillet over medium heat until golden brown. Remove with slotted spoon and transfer to 4-quart (4 L) Dutch oven. Add onion and shallot to skillet and brown quickly over high heat. Transfer to saucepan using slotted spoon.
- Coat beef cubes with flour, shaking off excess. Add butter to same skillet if necessary and melt over medium heat. Add meat in several batches and brown evenly on all sides. Add to saucepan containing pork, onions and shallots.
- Pour Cognac into hot skillet and cook until only a thin glaze of liquid remains. Stir in beef bouillon and bring to boil, scraping up any browned bits clinging to pan. Add to beef along with Dijon mustard and French mustard and reserved pork rind. Bring to simmer, cover partially and cook until beef is barely tender, about 2-3 hours.
- Add carrot and cook until fork tender. Season to taste with salt and pepper.
- Stew can be prepared to this point and frozen for up to 3 months.

DIJON AND COGNAC BEEF STEW (CONT'D.)

- Just before serving, bring stew to simmer.
- Heat remaining butter in medium skillet over medium heat. Add mushrooms and brown well. Add wine and remaining mustard and boil about 20 seconds. Stir mixture into stew and let simmer for 5 minutes.
- Serves 4-6.

AFRICAN BEEF STEW

A cookbook without a recipe which includes peanut butter, never! However, who has ever heard of peanut butter and beef? We have!

Ragout de boeuf a l'Africaine — African beef stew is an absolute must and certainly worthy of company coming consideration. And will you be in for a surprise, it won't be just the kids who are asking for repeats.

2½ lb.	*lean chuck steak or roast cut in 1" (2.5 cm) cubes	1.25 kg
2 tbsp.	vegetable oil	30 mL
3	onions, thinly sliced	3
3	carrots, thinly sliced	3
3	garlic cloves, minced	3
3 tbsp.	tomato paste	45 mL
¼ tsp.	ground cloves	1 mL
½ tsp.	ground ginger	2 mL
dash	cayenne pepper	dash
1 tbsp.	vinegar	15 mL
2 cups	water	500 mL
1	bay leaf	1
dash	salt	dash
dash	pepper	dash
¼ cup	peanut butter	50 mL
2 tbsp.	flour	30 mL
2 tbsp.	honey	30 mL

- In a heavy skillet heat the vegetable oil. Sauté beef until golden brown. Add onions, carrots and garlic, cook for 3 minutes.
- Add tomato paste, cloves, ginger, cayenne pepper, vinegar, water, bay leaf and salt and pepper to taste. Stir in peanut butter. Cover and cook over a gentle heat for 2½ hours.
- Remove 3 tbsp. (45 mL) of liquid from the casserole. Place in a small bowl and add flour and honey. Mix thoroughly. Add back to the casserole and stir until the sauce thickens.
- Serves 6.

OVEN-BAKED BEEF STEW

Beef stew with a difference! Herbs, vegetables, beef, gravy topped with dumplings made from refrigerated biscuits, rolled in crushed cornflakes and baked until they're golden brown. WOW! . . . seconds please!

1½ lbs.	*lean beef stew meat, in 1" (2.5 cm) cubes	750 g
¼ cup	all-purpose flour	50 mL
2 tsp.	salt	10 mL
dash	freshly ground pepper	dash
3-4	medium carrots, cut in 2" (5 cm) strips	3-4
4	small onions, quartered	4
½ cup	celery, thinly sliced	125 mL
2 cups	water	500 mL
5½ oz.	can tomato paste	156 mL
1 tbsp.	vinegar	15 mL
2 tbsp.	red wine	30 mL
1 tbsp.	soy sauce	15 mL
1 tsp.	sugar	5 mL
⅛ tsp.	dried thyme, crushed	0.5 mL
dash	basil	dash
1	garlic clove, minced	1
1	bay leaf	1
10 oz.	frozen peas and pods, broken apart	300 g
1 pkg.	refrigerator biscuits (6 biscuits)	1 pkg.
	milk	
¼ cup	crushed cornflakes	50 mL

- In a paper or plastic bag combine flour, salt and pepper. Add beef cubes, a few at a time; shake to coat. Place coated beef cubes in 3-quart (3 L) casserole; add carrots, onions and celery.
- In a bowl combine water, tomato paste, vinegar, wine, soy sauce, sugar, thyme, basil, garlic and bay leaf; pour over meat in casserole. Cover and bake in 350°F (180°C) oven for 2 hours.
- Stir frozen pea pods into stew mixture, cover and bake for 20 minutes longer. Remove casserole from oven; discard bay leaf. Increase oven temperature to 425°F (220°C).
- Meanwhile, quarter the refrigerator biscuits, dip each quarter in milk, then roll in crushed flakes. Place on top of stew.
- Bake, uncovered, in 425°F (220°C) oven for about 12 minutes or until biscuits are done.
- Serves 6.

BORSCH OVEN-BAKED STEW

One tends to think that a stew, is a stew, is a stew. Wrong! Depending on the ingredients added and the subsequent sauce — stews can taste very different. Our oven-baked Borsch stew is different not only in taste and texture but also in color. The rich color of sliced beets not only enhances the eye appeal of this serving but, at the same time, does great things for your taste buds. It might well be that they will go AWOL and only the promise of another serving will guarantee a return.

2 lbs.	*lean beef short ribs, cut in 1" (2.5 cm) cubes	1 kg
4	carrots, sliced	4
1½ cups	diced turnips	375 mL
3 stalks	celery, sliced	3 stalks
1	medium onion, sliced	1
4½ cups	water	1 L
5½ oz.	can tomato paste	156 mL
1 tsp.	salt	5 mL
½ tsp.	pepper	2 mL
1 cup	water	250 mL
1 tbsp.	sugar	15 mL
2 tbsp.	vinegar	30 mL
2	medium beets peeled, sliced and cut into strips	2
1	small head of cabbage chopped	1
1 cup	sour cream (optional)	250 mL

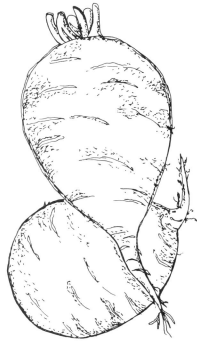

- Preheat oven to 350°F (180°C).
- All vegetables can be sliced in food processor on a medium cutter.
- Trim any excess fat from ribs. In a heavy 4-quart (4 L) pot or Dutch oven, brown ribs on all sides and drain. Add carrots, turnips, celery and onion.
- Blend 4½ cups (1 L) of water, tomato paste, salt and pepper; pour over meat and vegetables. Cover and bake at 350°F (180°C) for 2 hours. Skim off fat.
- Combine 1 cup (250 mL) of water, sugar and vinegar; stir into the meat mixture. Add the beets and cabbage. Cover and bake for an additional 1½ hours.
- Serves 6 with plenty of sour cream available for individual tastes.

BEEF POT PIE

Light and fluffy pastry . . . tasty vegetables simmered in a mellow wine sauce . . . voila! beef pot pie. We have so many fall, winter and spring days in Canada . . . and what could be more comforting on a crisp working day than to know that dinner includes a tossed salad, beef pie, a bottle of wine and best of all . . . good company.

Finish your dinner with feet up, FANTASTIC FINALE, page 139, and coffee.

1½ lbs.	*lean boneless beef chuck cut into 2" (5 cm) pieces	750 g
1 tbsp.	unsalted butter	15 mL
1 tbsp.	olive oil	15 mL
1	medium onion, coarsely chopped	1
2	garlic cloves, minced	2
2 tbsp.	unbleached, all-purpose flour	30 mL
1 tsp.	salt	5 mL
1 tsp.	freshly ground pepper	5 mL
2 cups	carrots in ½" (1 cm) slices	500 mL
5	small, new, red potatoes, cut into 8 pieces each	5
½ cup	chopped fresh parsley	125 mL
1 tbsp.	mustard, Dijon-style	15 mL
1 cup	dry red wine	250 mL
1 cup	beef bouillon (see page 148)	250 mL
½ cup	red wine vinegar	125 mL
1 tsp.	dried thyme	5 mL
2 tbsp.	dark brown sugar	30 mL
8 oz.	green beans, ends trimmed, cut in half	250 g
1	egg	1
1 tbsp.	water	15 mL

- Preheat oven to 350°F (180°C).
- In a heavy skillet, heat butter and oil over medium heat. Slowly add beef and brown evenly on all sides. Place beef in a medium-sized casserole.
- Sauté the onion and garlic in the same skillet for 2 minutes. Add to beef in smaller casserole.
- Mix the flour, salt and pepper and sprinkle over the beef, tossing to coat evenly.
- Add the carrots, potatoes, parsley, mustard, wine, bouillon, vinegar, thyme and brown sugar to the beef and stir to combine. Heat to boiling over medium heat. Cover and place in the oven. Bake for 1 hour. Remove the cover and bake for another 30 minutes.
- While the beef is baking, make the pastry (see opposite).

BEEF POT PIE (CONT'D.)

- Place the green beans and water to cover in a saucepan. Heat to boiling. Reduce heat and simmer for 5 minutes. Do not overcook beans.
- Remove the beef stew from the oven. Increase the heat to 425°F (220°C). Stir the beans into the stew, taste and adjust the seasonings.
- Mix the egg and water in a small bowl. Pour the beef stew into a 2" (5 cm) deep casserole or soufflé dish. Roll out the pastry and place on top of the dish. Trim the pastry, leaving a 1" (2.5 cm) border. Brush the edge of the dish with egg wash and press the overhang dough onto the dish. Crimp the pastry decoratively and brush the top with egg wash. Cut your initial in the center of the pastry as a steam vent.
- Place the beef pie on a baking sheet and bake on the middle rack until the crust is a delicious golden color, about 20-25 minutes. Serve immediately.
- Serves 6 very lucky people.

PASTRY . . . incredibly light and flaky.

1½ cups	sifted, unbleached flour	375 mL
½ tsp.	salt	2 mL
½ cup	unsalted butter, chilled and cut into small pieces	125 mL
¼ cup	ice water	50 mL

- Mix the flour and salt in a large mixing bowl. With a pastry blender cut in the butter until the mixture resembles peas.
- Add the ice water and blend into the flour mixture.
- Turn the dough out onto a lightly floured surface and knead 10-12 times.
- Shape the dough into a ball, wrap in waxed paper and refrigerate for at least 30 minutes before using.

FANTASTIC FINALE

- Toast as many slices of pound cake as required. (Set oven to broil temperature and place rack approximately 10" (25 cm) from heat).
- Add a scoop of ice cream, a sprinkle of Grand Marnier and a goodly amount of shaved chocolate. Your eating public will be convinced that something this good must have taken a very long time to prepare.

HUNGARIAN GOULASH with FETTUCCINI

Goulash conjures up an image of a busy family day. It seems to be the type of day one encounters about August 28th or 29th when every mother is trying to get the kids outfitted, booked and penciled, dentisted and finally, spiffed at the barbershop.

Busy days demand a one-dish meal that needs only whole-wheat dinner rolls and a light dessert before that final 'umph' and the settling process begins.

2 lbs.	*lean beef stew, cut in 1" (2.5 cm) cubes	1 kg
1	onion, coarsely chopped	1
1 tsp.	salt	5 mL
½ tsp.	freshly ground pepper	2 mL
¼ tsp.	celery salt	1 mL
¼ tsp.	garlic salt	1 mL
1½ tbsp.	paprika	22 mL
4	large tomatoes	4
1 cup	sour cream	250 mL

- Place beef, onion, salt, pepper, celery salt and paprika in 3-quart (3 L) microproof casserole.
- Peel and seed tomatoes. Cut into chunks. Add tomatoes and stir.
- Cook covered, on 70% POWER (Medium High) in microwave, 55-60 minutes, or until beef is tender, stirring twice during cooking. Stir sour cream gradually into mixture and let stand, covered for 5 minutes.
- Serve over buttered, seasoned fettuccini.
- Serves 4-6.
- Dieting? Substitute yogurt for sour cream.

SPEEDY SOUP à la BEEF

The one element that none can beg, borrow or steal, is time. And when you're short of time, you're short of time. So, we include this recipe, which is quick and easy and, at the same time, tasty enough to impress even finicky eaters.

1½ lb.	*lean beef blade or cross-rib roast or steak, excess fat removed	750 g
3½ cups	water	875 mL
1 cup	tomato juice	250 mL
1 lb.	tomatoes, canned or chopped fresh	500 g
10 oz.	frozen mixed vegetables	300 g
1 cup	frozen, loose-pack hash-brown potatoes	250 mL
¼ cup	onion soup mix	50 mL
¼ cup	thinly sliced celery	50 mL
1 tsp.	sugar	5 mL
1 tsp.	salt	5 mL
⅛ tsp.	celery salt	0.5 mL
½ tsp.	Worcestershire sauce	2 mL
dash	freshly ground pepper	dash
dash	Tabasco sauce	dash

- In a 3-quart (3 L) saucepan combine water, tomato juice and beef; bring to a boil. Reduce heat, cover and simmer for 2½ to 3 hours or until meat is tender.
- Remove soup from heat source. Extract beef with strainer. When beef is cool, remove meat from bones; cut into bite-sized pieces and momentarily set aside.
- Skim fat from surface of soup, or, if you have time, chill soup until fat congeals, making it very easy to remove excess.
- Return beef to soup mixture and bring to a boil. Add 'undrained' tomatoes, mixed vegetables, potatoes, dry onion soup mix, celery, sugar, salts, Worcestershire sauce, pepper, garlic and Tabasco sauce.
- Reduce heat, cover and simmer for 15 to 20 minutes or until vegetables are tender.
- Serves 6.

SOUP . . . SOUP . . . BEEF GOULASH SOUP

A loud ear splitting HURRAH for beef soup, the stuff which keeps so many Canadians going through our long, Illoooonnnng winters.

Beef goulash soup, available for grazing over the weekend when everyone is home or as an appetizer. Either way, try to have whole-wheat buns handy for making sure that every morsel is removed from the bottom of the bowl!

2 lbs.	*lean beef stew meat, cut in 1" (2.5 cm) cubes, fat removed	1 kg
4 slices	bacon	4 slices
2	onions, chopped	2
2	garlic cloves, minced	2
1-1½ tbsp.	paprika	15-22 mL
2 tsp.	salt	10 mL
1 tsp.	pepper, freshly ground	5 mL
1	medium tomato, chopped	1
5½ oz.	can tomato paste	156 mL
3	potatoes, peeled and finely chopped	3
2 cups	water	500 mL
½ cup	carrots, finely sliced	125 mL
½ cup	celery, finely chopped	125 mL

- In Dutch oven, cook bacon until crisp. Drain, reserve drippings; crumble bacon. Cook onions and garlic in reserved drippings until tender.
- Stir in paprika, salt and pepper. Add meat cubes and bacon, cook and stir 2 to 3 minutes.
- Add tomato, tomato paste and water. Cover and simmer 1¼ hours or until meat is nearly tender.
- Add potatoes, carrots and celery. Simmer 20 minutes. Remove any excess fat.
- Serves 6.

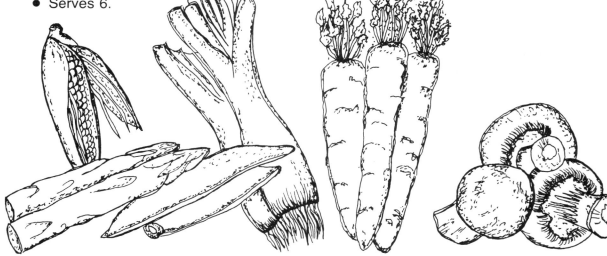

MEATY MINESTRONE

WATCH OUT, MR. CAMPBELL, here comes the great white soup brigade! Minestrone with vegetables and beef, perfect for a quick but satisfying meal, great for on the 'go'. Should you have leftovers, soup is great in a lunch thermos.

Great company . . . toasted cheese-bread allows for a quick 'dunk' and a sneaky slurp when no one is paying attention!

2 lbs.	*lean stewing beef	1 kg
1	medium onion, chopped	1
1	bay leaf	1
2 tsp.	salt	10 mL
1 tsp.	pepper	5 mL
¼ tsp.	beef bouillon granules	1 mL
dash	Italian seasoning	dash
8 cups	water	2 L
1 lb.	green beans, fresh, frozen	500 g
1 lb.	garbanzo beans, canned	500 g
½ lb.	fresh tomatoes	250 g
1 cup	carrots, thinly sliced	250 mL
2 stalks	celery, thinly sliced	2 stalks
4 oz.	Polish sausage, thinly sliced	125 g
2 oz.	fine egg noodles	55 g
2 tbsp.	parsley	30 mL
1	garlic clove, minced	1
1½ tsp.	dried basil	7 mL

- In Dutch oven combine beef, onion, bay leaf, salt, pepper, beef bouillon granules and Italian seasoning. Add water. Cover and simmer about 2 hours or until meat is tender. Remove beef and skim fat from both. Alternately, if you allow the mixture to cool, the excess will congeal and is then very easy to remove.
- Add green beans, garbanzo beans, tomatoes, carrots, celery, sausage, noodles, parsley, garlic and basil to soup. Cover and simmer for 20 to 25 minutes or until vegetables and noodles are tender.
- Remove bay leaf. Season to taste.
- Serves 8-10.

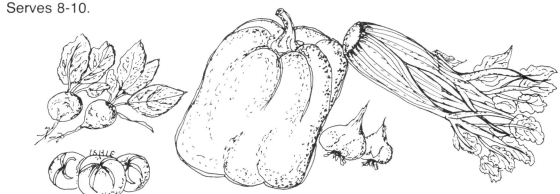

PEACH-GLAZED CORNED BEEF

Mellow the taste of corned beef with a light, colorful, delicately sweetened glaze and provide a culinary experience that few will have enjoyed before!

You may find, as we did, that doubling the glaze recipe is the 'United Nations' way to prevent arguments as to who has more than the next, or, in today's vernacular, who has 'pigged out.' 'Doubled' allows for everyone to be fully satisfied.

3 lbs.	*corned beef brisket	1.5 kg
2 cups	water	500 mL
4	small apples	4
½ cup	water	125 mL
⅓ cup	peach preserves	75 mL
¼ tsp.	ground ginger	1 mL

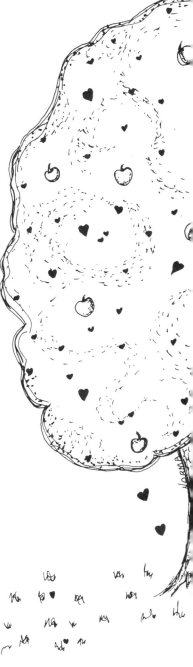

- Rinse brisket in cold water to remove pickling juices. Place on a rack in a shallow roasting pan, fat side up. Add 2 cups (500 mL) water. Cover with foil.
- Roast for 2 hours at 325°F (160°C). Uncover, drain cooking liquid and discard. Cut apples in half lengthwise and core. Arrange apple halves, skin side up, around corned beef in roasting pan, add ½ cup (125 mL) water to pan. Return to oven, continue roasting uncovered for an additional 30 minutes.
- Combine peach preserves and ground ginger. Turn apple halves skin side down. Spoon peach glaze over apple halves and corned beef, return to oven and cook until glaze is hot, about 15 minutes longer.
- Serves 6.

SAUERKRAUT AND BRISKET OF BEEF

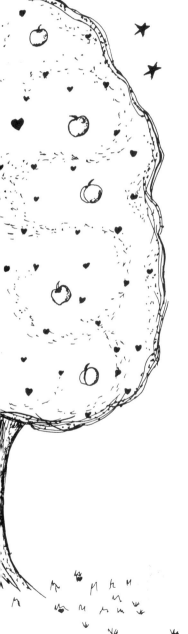

A traditional recipe enjoyed for many years, especially among European families. You will understand why, when, along with beef and sauerkraut, you serve parslied potatoes, fresh green peas and crunchy dinner rolls.

Dessert? Of course . . . cut a pound cake in half, fill center with butter pecan ice cream and dazzle your family with a drizzle of 4 melted squares of semisweet chocolate over the top.

3 lbs.	*lean beef brisket	1.5 kg
1	large onion, diced	1
to taste	salt	to taste
3 cups	sauerkraut	750 mL
1	large potato, grated	1
1	tart, red apple, quartered, cored but not peeled	1
1 tsp.	caraway seeds	5 mL
1 cup	dry red wine	250 mL

- In a 5-quart (5 L) pot, place the brisket and diced onion. Salt to taste.
- Cover with boiling water, cover and bring to a hard boil. Boil for 20 minutes, skim off fat, re-cover and simmer for 1 hour.
- Remove the meat and slice **against** the grain into ¼" (6 mm) pieces. Reserve ½ cup (125 mL) of pot liquid.
- Return the meat to the pot with ½ cup (125 mL) of pot liquid; add the sauerkraut, grated potato, quartered apple and caraway seeds. Bring to a boil, cover, reduce the heat and simmer for another ½ hour.
- Add wine and simmer until the meat is tender, about 15-30 minutes.
- Serves 6.

LIVER CREOLE

Creoles, Louisiana-born descendents of French settlers, have made a significant contribution to the culinary culture of this continent.

Creole cooking . . . imaginative, colorful, zippy and usually hotly spiced. Sooooo hot that it has, over the years, tempted many to stash away a few more bites than originally intended.

Beef liver is a fantastic source of iron, especially needed by women. Unfortunately, when measured on a scale of 1 to 10 in taste, it is usually found somewhere in the bottom one-third.

We offer **LIVER CREOLE** in the belief that this pleasurable Creole rendition will not only overcome most objections but will probably generate some converts!

1½ lbs.	calf liver, thinly sliced	750 g
¾ cup	flour	175 mL
½ tsp.	salt	2 mL
dash	pepper, freshly ground	dash
4 tbsp.	butter	60 mL

- During last 7 minutes of cooking time for sauce, combine flour, salt and pepper on a plate. Thoroughly coat liver with flour.
- Heat butter in frying pan. Add floured liver and quickly brown on both sides, approximately 2 minutes per side. Do not overcook or liver will become tough.
- Serve at once with sauce.
- Serves 4-5.

SAUCE

2 cups	tomato juice	500 mL
1	medium onion, chopped	1
2	small green onions, chopped	2
1	green pepper, chopped	1
¼ tsp.	salt	1 mL
dash	pepper, freshly ground	dash
1 tsp.	Worcestershire sauce	5 mL
¼ tsp.	garlic salt	1 mL
½ tsp.	celery seed	2 mL
1 tbsp.	chopped parsley	15 mL
¼ lb.	washed mushrooms, chopped	125 g

- Combine all sauce ingredients except mushrooms. Bring to a boil, reduce heat and simmer, uncovered for about 25 minutes, stirring occasionally. Add mushrooms and simmer 2 or 3 minutes longer.

BAKED STUFFED HEART

Stuffed heart is a delicacy which, unfortunately, is unfamiliar, especially among the younger generation.

Slowly cooked beef heart — filled with a savory dressing is a most pleasant change from the everyday dinner fare.

Surprise someone . . . try stuffed heart!

2½ lbs.	beef heart	1.2 kg approx.
2 tbsp.	butter	30 mL
1	small onion, chopped	1
¼ cup	chopped celery	50 mL
¼ tsp.	oregano	1 mL
¼ tsp.	celery seed	1 mL
½ tsp.	salt	2 mL
¼ tsp.	pepper	1 mL
2 or 3 slices	bread, cubed	2 or 3 slices

- Wash heart thoroughly. Trim all fat and remove arteries and veins.
- Melt butter in skillet, add onion, celery, oregano, celery seed salt and pepper. Sauté gently for 3 minutes.
- Remove from heat and stir in bread crumbs. Fill heart cavity with stuffing. Tie snugly with string.
- Bake covered in oven for 2½ hours at 300°F (150°C).
- Slice into ½" (1 cm) slices.
- Wild Rice Gourmet, page 161, fresh asparagus and warmed, crusty rolls will leave your dinner companions feeling that, whatever transpired that day wasn't so bad when viewed from the other side of a satisfying dinner!
- Serves 4-6.

BEEF BOUILLON

4 lbs.	beef bones with meat	2 kg
3 quarts	water	3 L
½ cup	sliced onion	125 mL
½ cup	diced carrots	125 mL
½ cup	diced celery and leaves	125 mL
½ cup	diced turnips	125 mL
2-3 sprigs	parsley	2-3 sprigs
1	small bay leaf	1
2 sprigs	marjoram	2 sprigs
8	whole black peppers	8
1 tbsp.	salt	15 mL

- Remove meat from bones and cut into small pieces. Put half the meat in soup kettle and add water, let stand 30 minutes.
- Scrape marrow from bones and melt; add remaining meat and brown on all sides. Add browned meat and bones to kettle; cook slowly 3 hours.
- Add vegetables and seasonings; continue cooking 2 hours. Strain and re-frigerate. Makes 2 quarts (2 L) stock.

IN A HURRY?
Beef consommé soup can be used in recipes calling for beef bouillon.

OUT OF SOUP?
1 beef bouillon cube dissolved in 1 cup (250 mL) boiling water may be used in recipes calling for beef bouillon.

COMPLIMENTARY
COMPLEMENTS FOR BEEF

- SALADS

- VEGETABLES

- DESSERTS

HAIL CAESAR the SUPREME SALAD

Nothing adds to a serving of beef quite like a spectacular salad! And nothing is more spectacular than the King of Salads, Caesar!.

1	large romaine head	1
1	garlic clove, halved	1
½ cup	olive oil	125 mL
1 cup	French bread cubes, ½'' (1 cm)	250 mL
¾ tsp.	salt	3 mL
¼ tsp.	dry mustard	1 mL
¼ tsp.	freshly ground black pepper	1 mL
1½ tsp.	Worcestershire sauce	7 mL
6	anchovy fillets, drained and chopped	6
1	egg, coddled	1
2 tbsp.	grated Parmesan cheese	30 mL
¼ cup	crumbled blue cheese (optional)	50 mL
½	lemon, juice of	½

- Trim, separate and wash romaine. Pat dry on paper towelling. Place romaine in plastic bag and refrigerate for several hours until crisp.
- Several hours before serving, crush ½ garlic clove and combine with salad oil in jar. Refrigerate, tightly covered for at least 1 hour.
- Preheat oven to 300°F (150°F). Heat 2 tbsp. (30 mL) oil-garlic mixture in shallow pan. Toast bread cubes for 20 minutes, or until golden brown. Toss often with fork.
- To remaining oil-garlic mixture add salt, mustard, pepper, Worcestershire and chopped anchovies. Shake vigorously and refrigerate.
- To coddle egg bring 2'' (5 cm) of water to boil in a small saucepan. Remove from heat. Carefully immerse egg into water and let stand for 1 minute. Remove and allow to cool.
- With remaining garlic clove, rub inside of salad bowl. Discard garlic. Rip romaine into large bite-sized pieces. Shake dressing and drizzle gently until each leaf glistens. Sprinkle with Parmesan. If using blue cheese as well, gently toss until all Romaine is evenly coated.

HAIL CAESAR the SUPREME SALAD (CONT'D.)

- You might save the last steps to perform at the dinner table as did the originator of this salad, Caesar, a Tijuana restauranteur. With panache, break the egg over the center of the salad. Pour lemon juice directly over egg and toss well. Flip the sautéed bread cubes over the top and, with great abandon, quickly toss again and serve all those faces which are wearing a smile that introduces one ear to the other!
- Serves 4-6.

CUCUMBER IN SOUR CREAM OR YOGURT

1	cucumber, peeled, thinly sliced	1
1 tsp.	salt	5 mL
1 tsp.	apple cider vinegar	5 mL
1 tsp.	fresh lemon juice	5 mL
1 tsp.	chopped, fresh chives	5 mL
1-1½ cups	sour cream or yogurt	250-375 mL

- Sprinkle cucumber with salt and apple cider vinegar. Cover and refrigerate for 1 hour or more.
- Drain. Combine remaining ingredients and fold in cucumber. Chill.
- Serves 4.

MARINATED BEAN SALAD

'Perk up' any dinner with an offering of bean salad. Its zest and crispness makes it an ideal companion for almost any beef serving.

Another nice thing about marinated bean salad . . . it can be made 1 or even 2 days in advance of serving.

2 x 19 oz.	cans chick peas, well-drained	2 x 540 mL
2 x 19 oz.	cans green lima beans, well-drained	2 x 540 mL
2 x 19 oz.	cans red kidney beans, well-drained	2 x 540 mL
19 oz.	can lentils, well-drained	540 mL
19 oz.	can green beans, well-drained	540 mL
19 oz.	can yellow beans, well-drained	540 mL
1	cauliflower, broken in small florets	1
1 lb.	mushrooms, quartered	500 g
4	carrots, cut into julienne strips	4
2	onions, thinly sliced	2
2	green peppers, halved, seeded and thinly sliced	2

DRESSING

2 tbsp.	chopped fresh parsley	30 mL
1 tsp.	dried basil	5 mL
2 tsp.	dry mustard	10 mL
1 tsp.	dried tarragon	5 mL
1 tsp.	salt	5 mL
¼ tsp.	freshly ground pepper	1 mL
¼ cup	sugar	50 mL
1 cup	red wine vinegar	250 mL
⅔ cup	vegetable oil	150 mL

- Combine vegetables in a large bowl.
- Combine dressing ingredients in small bowl; mix well. Pour dressing over vegetables, coating well. Allow vegetables to marinate, covered, in refrigerator at least overnight or up to 2 days.
- Taste just before serving and adjust seasonings if necessary.
- Serves 10-12.

ORANGE AND CELERY SALAD

A refreshingly different salad. Colorful and crisp with the ability to cleanse the palate while awaiting the promise of beef 'par excellence'.

4	oranges, peeled and separated	4
1 stalk	celery, thinly sliced	1 stalk
1	mild onion, coarsely chopped	1
1 tsp.	coriander seeds, lightly crushed	5 mL
2 tbsp.	red wine vinegar	30 mL
OR		
	lemon juice	
5 tbsp.	olive oil	75 mL
	salt	
	freshly ground pepper	
	celery leaves, to garnish	

- Place the orange segments, celery and onion in a salad bowl. Toss lightly to mix. Sprinkle with the coriander seeds. Combine all the dressing ingredients and mix thoroughly. Pour over salad and toss gently. Garnish with celery leaves.
- Serves 4.

FRENCH SALAD BOWL
WITH BACON AND SPINACH

Profundo basso! Variation on a theme, French dressing, an unexpected treat in a spinach salad.

6	garlic cloves, quartered	6
¾ cup	French dressing	175 mL
9 cups	spinach	2 L
3	eggs, hard-cooked	3
8	bacon slices, cooked	8

- Add garlic to French dressing; cover and refrigerate for 3 hours. In salad bowl, tear spinach into pieces, cover and refrigerate.
- Chop eggs, crumble bacon, sprinkle both over spinach. Remove garlic from dressing, then pour over salad. Toss thoroughly and serve at once.
- Serves 6.

PEPPERONI PASTA SALAD

A salad with panache! Pepperoni Pasta Salad looks so very colorful and inviting. Thin, slender cuts of zucchini, peppers and noodles amidst olives and onions.

½ lb.	rotini noodles	250 g
2 tbsp.	olive oil	30 mL
1	small red pepper, cut in julienne strips	1
1	small green pepper, cut in julienne strips	1
3 oz.	pepperoni, cut in julienne strips	85 g
1	tomato, coarsely chopped	1
1 cup	zucchini, unpeeled, julienned	250 mL
½ cup	mushroom caps	125 mL
¾ cup	white Cheddar cheese	175 mL
½ cup	coarsely chopped parsley	125 mL
½ cup	Greek olives	125 mL
½ cup	finely chopped red onion	125 mL

DRESSING

6 tbsp.	olive oil	90 mL
2 tbsp.	red wine vinegar	30 mL
1	garlic clove, minced	1
2 tsp.	dried basil	10 mL
½ tsp.	salt	2 mL
¼ tsp.	dried oregano	1 mL
to taste	freshly ground pepper	to taste

- Cook noodles according to package directions or until tender, but still firm, al dente. Drain. Rinse under cold running water and drain well.
- Transfer to salad bowl and toss with 2 tbsp. (30 mL) olive oil. Add peppers, pepperoni, tomato, zucchini, mushroom caps, cheese, parsley, olives and onions. Toss lightly to mix.
- Combine all dressing ingredients; mix thoroughly. Pour over salad and toss. Cover and refrigerate until serving time.
- Serves 6-8.

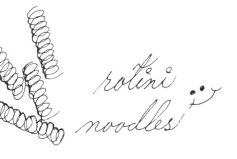

rotini noodles

GREEN GODDESS SALAD

San Franciscans, we're told, were the first to enjoy this unique salad. We tip our hats and say 'thank you' for sharing a good thing. Try it and you will understand why it has found its way 'round the world.

1	garlic clove, minced	1
½ tsp.	salt	2 mL
½ tsp.	dry mustard	2 mL
1 tsp.	Worcestershire sauce	5 mL
2 tbsp.	anchovy paste	30 mL
3 tbsp.	tarragon wine vinegar	45 mL
3 tbsp.	minced chives or minced green onions	45 mL
⅓ cup	chopped parsley	75 mL
1 cup	mayonnaise	250 mL
½ cup	sour cream	125 mL
dash	freshly ground pepper	dash
1 quart	salad greens	1 L
	stuffed olives, for garnish	

- Combine all ingredients except salad greens and olives early in the day. Mix thoroughly, cover and refrigerate until needed. Makes about 1⅓ cups (325 mL) dressing.
- To serve: place salad greens in bowl. Pour about ⅓ of the dressing over them. Mix thoroughly and serve immediately. Garnish with stuffed olives.
- Serves 4.

SIPPETS

Sippets were introduced in the early 19th century by Meg Dods. She recognized the need for 'something' that would carefully collect all those little bits of fantastic flavor left behind. 'Sippets,' she said, 'are the answer'. Simply brown slices of bread in butter and after draining them on towelling, they're perfect for collecting tender morsels of food.

TOMATOES WITH HORSERADISH SAUCE

Horseradish with beef ... an all-time favorite. Offer this mellow Horse-radish Sauce spooned over the clean, bright taste of cherry tomatoes for an interesting change of pace.

1 lb.	small cherry tomatoes, skinned	500 g
⅔ cup	mayonnaise	150 mL
4 tbsp.	sour cream	60 mL
4 tbsp.	plain yogurt, unsweetened	60 mL
2 tsp.	lemon juice	10 mL
4 tbsp.	grated horseradish	60 mL
1-1½ tbsp.	chopped fresh dill	15-22 mL
1 sprig	dill, for garnish	1 sprig

- In a bowl combine mayonnaise with sour cream and yogurt. Add the lemon juice, horseradish and dill. Stir.
- Place the tomatoes in a pyramid on a flat serving dish.
- Spoon the Horseradish Sauce over the tomatoes just before serving and garnish with the dill sprig.
- Serves 4.

TOMATO AND BASIL SALAD

BON APPÉTIT — marinated tomatoes and basil. A delicious combination providing a perfect appetizer or a refreshing accompaniment with the main course.

1½ lbs.	large tomatoes, sliced	750 g
to taste	freshly ground black pepper	to taste
½ tsp.	sugar	2 mL
3 tbsp.	olive oil	45 mL
1 tbsp.	white wine vinegar	15 mL
2 tbsp.	thin strips fresh basil	30 mL
1 sprig	basil, for garnish	1 sprig
6 oz.	mozzarella cheese, thinly sliced (optional)	170 g

- Arrange the tomato slices, neatly overlapping, on a large flat serving dish. Season with plenty of pepper and sprinkle with sugar.
- Combine the oil and vinegar, spoon evenly over the tomatoes. Refrigerate, covered for 1 hour.
- Sprinkle with thin strips of basil just before serving. Add basil sprig garnish.
- Looking for a light lunch, add 6 oz. (170 g) mozzarella cheese, thinly sliced.
- Serves 4.

TOMATO ASPIC

Tomato aspic with its fresh, clean, bright taste stands unchallenged as the most refreshing condiment to serve with almost any beef dish.

1¾ cup	tomato juice	425 mL
¼ cup	vinegar	50 mL
½ tsp.	Worcestershire sauce	2 mL
2 tbsp.	unflavored gelatin	30 mL
¼ cup	water	50 mL
3 tbsp.	lemon juice	45 mL
½ cup	celery, finely chopped	125 mL
4 oz.	can shrimp, small	125 g
1 tbsp.	onion	15 mL

- Bring tomato juice, vinegar and Worcestershire to boil. Soften gelatin in cold water; add to hot tomato mixture. Add lemon juice.
- Place in refrigerator. Cool and allow to set to the point that the gelatin will hold solids. Add celery, shrimp and onion.
- Spoon gelatin mixture into jelly mold. Cover and refrigerate.
- Unmold tomato aspic onto serving platter; tuck lettuce leaves under for garnish.
- Serves 6-8.
- Company company? This recipe can be doubled to serve a larger group of guests.
- In a hurry, lemon Jell-o may be substituted in place of gelatin. Use a 3 oz. (85 g) package of Jell-o, add to hot tomato mixture, mixing to thoroughly dissolve all granules. Follow rest of directions.

HONEY-GLAZED SHALLOTS WITH MINT

If real men don't eat quiche, then they must eat shallots, mellowed with honey and, for good measure, a parting shot of mint.

1¼ lb.	shallots, remove tips, root ends and papery skin, leaving only the cloves	625 g
1 tbsp.	salted butter	15 mL
1 tbsp.	honey	15 mL
dash	salt	dash
dash	freshly ground black pepper	dash
1 cup	chicken bouillon**	250 mL
1 tbsp.	mint, chopped fresh or dried	15 mL

- In a heavy skillet large enough to hold the shallots in a single layer, melt the butter over medium heat.
- Stir in the honey and add the shallots, salt and pepper. Pour in the bouillon and bring the liquid to a simmer.
- Cook until almost all the liquid has evaporated — about 30 minutes.
- Stir in the mint.
- Serves 4.

**If you don't have chicken broth, dissolve 1 chicken bouillon cube in 1 cup (250 mL) of boiling water.

MEAT LOAF en CROÛTE

SOUR CREAM PASTRY FOR YOUR FAVORITE MEAT LOAF

2½ cups	all-purpose flour	625 mL
½ tsp.	salt	2 mL
1 cup	butter	250 mL
½ cup	sour cream	125 mL
1	egg	1

- Work flour, salt and butter with fingers until mixture has the consistency of coarse meal. Mix sour cream with egg, then stir into flour and butter, working it into a ball with your fingers. Wrap in waxed paper and refrigerate 1 hour.
- Using your favorite meat loaf recipe, form a loaf that will fit into a 9 x 5 x 3" (23 x 12 x 7 cm) pan and place in the refrigerator for approximately 1 hour to chill.
- Roll out pastry to fit a 9 x 5 x 3" (2 L or 23 x 12 x 7 cm) loaf pan. Place your favorite meat loaf mixture on top of rolled pastry and brush edges of pastry with some of the egg-cream mixture. Cover top of meat loaf with pastry, press edges together.
- Brush top and edges with egg-cream mixture. If desired, decorate the top of pastry, then prick top to allow steam to escape. Bake in the center of a 375°F (190°C) oven 45 minutes or until golden brown.

NOODLES CARAWAY

4 quarts	water	4 L
1 tbsp.	salt	15 mL
½ lb.	wide egg noodles	250 g
	onion, chopped	
3 tbsp.	butter	45 mL
1 tsp.	caraway seed	5 mL
	salt	
	freshly ground pepper	

- In a large saucepan bring water and salt to boil. Add noodles and cook until tender but firm, al dente. Drain, rinse with warm water and drain again.
- Melt butter in same pan over medium heat. Add onion and sauté until soft. Stir in caraway and cook about 1 minute. Add noodles, tossing to heat through. Season to taste with salt and pepper. Remove to heated serving bowl.
- Serves 4.

POTATO PETALS

6	baking potatoes, scrubbed	6
1	garlic clove, chopped	1
1 tbsp.	olive oil	15 mL
2	egg whites, lightly beaten	2
¼ tsp.	nutmeg	1 mL
¼ tsp.	salt	1 mL
¼ tsp.	freshly ground pepper	1 mL
½ cup	plain yogurt	125 mL
2 tbsp.	finely chopped chives	30 mL

- After baking the potatoes for about 1½ hours or until tender, scoop out the centers and press through a sieve.
- Combine the garlic and oil in a small saucepan over medium heat. Cook for 2 minutes and then add to potatoes.
- Add egg white, nutmeg, salt, pepper and mix well.
- Form the mixture into 10-12 mounds about 2" (5 cm) in diameter and make an indentation in the top of each with the back of spoon. Place on a greased cooking sheet.
- Bake the potato petals for 7-10 minutes at 400°F (200°C) or until edges are crisp and brown.
- Combine the yogurt and chives in a small bowl. At the last moment add this mixture to the center of each potato petal and serve this delicious combination!

YELLOW RICE

2½ cups	water	625 mL
1 tbsp.	butter	15 mL
1 cup	rice	250 mL
1 tbsp.	brown sugar	15 mL
1	cinnamon stick	1
1 tsp.	salt	5 mL
½ cup	seeded raisins	125 mL
1 tsp.	turmeric	5 mL

- Bring water to a boil and add butter. Place all remaining ingredients in water and stir for first minute. Cover.
- Allow rice to cook slowly over low heat until all water is absorbed, about 40 minutes.
- Remove cinnamon stick and serve.
- Serves 4.

WILD RICE GOURMET

A dish meant to complement any beef serving. Wild rice cooked in a delicate blend of herbs offers plenty of room for superlatives such as, great, wonderful or just plain terrific!

1 cup	uncooked wild rice	250 mL
3 cups	boiling water	750 mL
1 tsp.	salt	5 mL
2 tbsp.	butter	30 mL
¼ cup	minced onion	50 mL
2 tbsp.	minced green pepper	30 mL
3-4 oz.	fresh sliced mushrooms	85-125 g
10 oz.	can cream of mushroom soup	284 mL
1 cup	heavy (whipping) cream	250 mL
¼ tsp.	dried marjoram	1 mL
dash	dried basil	dash
dash	dried tarragon	dash
½ tsp.	curry powder	2 mL
½ tsp.	salt	2 mL
¼ tsp.	pepper	1 mL

- 40 minutes before serving, wash rice in cold water. Add rinsed rice to boiling water. Add 1 tsp. (5 mL) salt. Cover, simmer for 30 minutes or until rice is tender.
- Melt butter in skillet and sauté onion, green pepper and mushrooms for 3 minutes. Stir in undiluted soup, cream, marjoram, basil, tarragon, curry powder, salt and pepper. Cook over medium heat for 10 minutes.
- Add cooked rice; heat for an additional 10 minutes, stirring occasionally.
- Serves 4.

ALBERTA BAKED BEANS

Alberta — the center of Canada's cattle country, where the cowboys roam, the quality of beef is unsurpassed and where you will find the very best baked beans in the world!!

The beans soak overnight and bake all day, producing a taste that makes one, even with the first mouthful, sit back and imagine the bawling of calves, the slow settling of dust, silent spurs and the lonely, penetrating, soul lifting, sounds of a harmonica as it renders its desired effect of quietening both stock and man.

1 lb.	pea or navy beans	500 g
2 tbsp.	dry mustard	30 mL
¼ tsp.	pepper	1 mL
1 tbsp.	salt	15 mL
3	medium onions, quartered	3
¼ cup	tightly packed brown sugar	50 mL
¼ cup	molasses	50 mL
1 cup	ketchup	250 mL
2 tbsp.	red wine vinegar	30 mL
dash	cloves	dash
¼ lb.	salt pork	125 g

- Remove any spoiled beans. Wash and place in large pot. Cover with 3 cups (750 mL) water; soak 8 hours or overnight.
- Add 2 additional cups (500 mL) of water to beans. Add other ingredients except salt pork. Boil, covered for 1 hour, or until skins wrinkle.
- Preheat oven to 250°F (120°C). Cut salt pork almost all the way through at ½" (1 cm) intervals. Place in large pot; add hot beans and their liquid, covering pork. Sprinkle with pepper.
- Bake 6 hours, covered, or until beans are tender.
- At the 4 hour mark, add about ¾ cup (175 mL) water, or enough to just cover. Uncover pot for the last ½ hour.
- Serves 4-6 or 3 hungry Alberta cowboys!

BANANAS ROYALE

2 tbsp.	butter	30 mL
3 tbsp.	maple syrup	45 mL
4	bananas, peeled, cut in bite-sized slices	4
2 tbsp.	lemon juice	30 mL

- In a small microproof dish, cook butter on 100% POWER (High) for 30 seconds or until butter is melted. Stir in maple syrup.
- Place bananas in dish and thoroughly coat with mixture. Cook at 100% POWER (High) for 1 minute. Stir bananas and cook an additional 1½ minutes at 100% POWER (High).
- Sprinkle with lemon juice and serve warm.
- Serves 4.

BAKED APPLE

4	large apples	4
3 tbsp.	brown sugar	45 mL
½ tsp.	cinnamon	2 mL
⅛ tsp.	nutmeg	0.5 mL
3 tbsp.	butter	45 mL
2 tsp.	golden raisins	10 mL

- Wash and core apples. Place in a circle in small microproof dish. Sprinkle brown sugar, cinnamon, nutmeg in center of each apple. Place a small amount of butter on top of each apple.
- Cover and cook at 100% POWER (High) for 3 minutes. Uncover and add raisins; rewrap and cook at same temperature for an additional 2 minutes.
- Serves 4.
- Goes down smoothly with a manly serving of ice cream!

FRUIT PIZZA

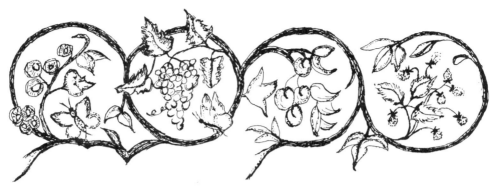

CRUST

3¼ cups	all-purpose flour	800 mL
1½ cups	sugar	375 mL
⅔ cup	butter	150 mL
2	eggs	2
2½ tsp.	double acting baking powder	12 mL
2 tbsp.	milk	30 mL
1 tsp.	vanilla	5 mL
½ tsp.	salt	2 mL

CUSTARD

8 oz.	cream cheese, softened	250 g
⅓ cup	granulated sugar	75 mL
	fruit topping, see below	

FRUIT GLAZE

½ cup	water	125 mL
½ cup	orange juice	125 mL
½ cup	sugar	125 mL
1½ tbsp.	cornstarch	22 mL
dash	salt	dash

- For crust, combine all ingredients in a large bowl. With mixer at medium setting, beat until well mixed, occasionally scraping bowl. Shape into a ball and then press on bottom of pizza pan. Bake at 350°F (180°C) for about 10 to 12 minutes or until golden brown. Cool.
- To make custard, beat cheese and sugar until soft. Spread over crust.
- For topping, use your imagination! Get wild! Color on color, fruit on fruit, kiwi and orange slices, bananas, fresh strawberries, blueberries, more kiwi fruit, peaches, apricots, cherry halves, something for everyone. Just arrange fruit in a circular pattern around the top. Canned fruit may be used, but your pizza will not be as crisp.
- Mix together the glaze ingredients. Cook until bubbly and glaze thickens. Pour over pizza.
- A garnish of whipped cream may be used when serving.
- See photograph, page 64.

EGGS à la NEIGE

A perfect companion for Beef Wellington, Eggs à la Neige, a famous specialty of New York City's Ritz-Carlton Hotel. Memories of magnificent days gone by linger with the enjoyment offered by this dessert of meringue nestled between layers of fresh strawberries and custard and sprinkled with chocolate!

4 cups	milk	1 L
6	eggs, separated	6
1¼ cups	sugar	300 mL
¼ tsp.	salt	1 mL
1½ cups	whipping cream	375 mL
¾ tsp.	vanilla	3 mL
1½ tbsp.	flour	22 mL
5 cups	sliced fresh strawberries	1.25 L
2	unsweetened squares chocolate	2

- Early in the day scald milk in large skillet. Beat egg whites until light and frothy. Gradually add ¾ cup (175 mL) sugar and salt; beating until stiff. Drop 3 large mounds of meringue into hot milk, 1" (2.5 cm) apart. Cook 5 minutes, turning once with a slotted spoon. Place meringues on paper towelling to drain. Repeat. Cover meringues and refrigerate. Reserve milk.
- In double boiler, scald cream with vanilla and 1½ cups (375 mL) reserved milk.
- In a small bowl beat egg yolks until light. Add ½ cup (125 mL) sugar, dash of salt, flour and a little of cream-milk mixture. Stir this back into the mixture in double boiler. Cook over hot, not boiling, water. Stir until sauce coats metal spoon. Cover and refrigerate.
- Just before serving your 'Pièce de Résistance', place strawberries in deep serving dish. Carefully heap the chilled meringues on top and finally pour on custard sauce. Shave and sprinkle oodles and oodles of chocolate on top.
- Serves 8 incredibly lucky people.
- See photograph, page 128.

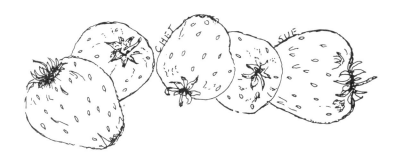

ORANGE MOUSSE

6	egg yolks	6
¼ cup	sugar	50 mL
1 tsp.	cornstarch	5 mL
3 tbsp.	water	45 mL
1 tbsp.	powdered gelatin	15 mL
1¾ cups	cream	425 mL
1 tbsp.	orange juice	15 mL
1	orange, thinly sliced, for garnish	1

- Bring a small amount of water to simmer in the bottom of a double boiler.
- In the top of the double boiler, mix egg yolks, sugar and cornstarch. Whisk until the mixture is thick and pale.
- Put 3 tbsp. (45 mL) of water in a small saucepan and sprinkle the gelatin over. Leave for a few minutes until spongy, then melt over a very gentle heat . . . make sure this mixture **does not** boil. Gently add to egg yolk mixture.
- Bring the cream to just below boiling point and whisk into the egg yolk mixture. Add orange juice.
- Pour into individual dessert dishes and chill for 2-3 hours or until set. Decorate mousse with twisted orange slices and a sugar wafer cookie.
- Serves 4.

BUTTER TART SLICE

CRUST

½ cup	butter	125 mL
2 tbsp.	sugar	30 mL
1½ cups	all-purpose flour	375 mL

BUTTER TART FILLING

2	eggs	2
1½ cups	brown sugar	375 mL
¼ cup	butter, melted	50 mL
1 tbsp.	vinegar	15 mL
1 cup	raisins	250 mL
1 tsp.	vanilla	5 mL

- Mix crust ingredients and press into a 9" x 9" (2.5 L) pan. Bake 5 minutes at 350°F (180°C).
- Mix filling thoroughly and pour over baked crust.
- Bake at 350°F (180°C) for 30-35 minutes. Yummmmmmmmy!

ROTE GRÜTZE

Rote Grütze is a classic German specialty . . . simple fare appealing to young and old alike. It is a wonderfully refreshing, light dessert.

1 lb. 10 oz.	fresh or frozen berries (blackberries, strawberries, raspberries, red currants, blueberries)	800 g
1 cup	dry red wine	250 mL
3 tbsp.	cornstarch	45 mL
¼ cup	sugar	50 mL
1 tbsp.	lemon juice, fresh	15 mL
1 piece	colored lemon peel lime peel, thinly curled for garnish	1 piece

- If fresh, rinse berries in cold water and drain thoroughly. Remove stems and hulls. Quarter strawberries.

- Stir together 3 tbsp. (45 mL) wine and cornstarch to make smooth paste.

- Combine remaining wine with sugar, lemon juice and lemon peel in large non-aluminum saucepan and bring to boil.

- Stir in cornstarch mixture and simmer over low heat for 5 minutes. Discard lemon peel. Add berries to liquid and return to boil.

- Spoon into 4 dessert dishes, cover and chill for 3-4 hours. Just before serving add a twist of lime peel for garnish.

- Serve with chilled whipping cream — **do not** whip cream . . . serve as a heavy cream.

- Serves 4.

MISSISSIPPI MUD

We hope that the name tweaks your curiosity much like it did ours. Imagine a dessert named Mississippi Mud. Only the most imaginative would give it a try after that handle. Once you have tried it you will probably become a 'mud' devotee.

BASE

1½ cups	all-purpose flour	375 mL
½ cup	butter	125 mL
2 tbsp.	ice water	30 mL
½ cup	crushed almonds	125 mL

FILLING I

8 oz.	cream cheese	250 g
1 cup	Cool Whip	250 mL
1 cup	icing sugar	250 mL

FILLING II

2 x 3½ oz.	pkg. instant chocolate pudding mix	2 x 100 g
3 cups	cold milk	750 mL
1 tsp.	vanilla	5 mL
	grated semisweet chocolate	

- Mix base as you would a pastry. Bake in 9" x 13" (22 x 33 cm) pan for 25 minutes at 350°F (180°C).
- Cream the cream cheese. Add Cool Whip and icing sugar and mix thoroughly. Spread over cooled crust.
- Mix ingredients for second filling thoroughly and let stand until thickened. Pour over cheese mixture.
- Use remaining Cool Whip and spread over chocolate pudding.
- Sprinkle with grated semisweet chocolate. Refrigerate.
- Serves 6-8.

YOUR GUIDE TO THE BEST OF BEEF

TODAY'S BEEF: NOW 35% LEANER

Agriculture Canada recently commissioned a study which shows that Canadian-produced *LEAN beef has an average 35% less fat than current nutrition tables indicate.

Unfortunately, for many years Canadian nutrition tables relied on beef data collected in the U.S. Since U.S. beef is fatter than Canadian beef, the tables overestimate the amount of fat Canadians obtain from beef.

Canadian producers have, since 1972, through improved production techniques, produced much leaner cattle.

YOUR NOTES

Tracy

Karen

Hope you enjoy!

SHARE THE "BEEF RENAISSANCE" WITH A FRIEND

BEEF — LIGHT, LEAN BEEF RECIPES
FOR CONTEMPORARY LIFESTYLES

Please send me _____ copies of "**BEEF**" at $12.95 per book plus $1.50 (total order) for postage and handling:

Enclosed is $_____.

NAME: _____

STREET: _____

CITY:_____ PROVINCE/STATE: _____

POSTAL CODE/ZIP: _____

Please make cheques or money orders payable to:
C & B Communications Ltd.
Karen Chase
R.R. #8
Calgary, Alberta
Canada   T2J 2T9

American Orders please pay in U.S. funds
Price is subject to change

SHARE THE "BEEF RENAISSANCE" WITH A FRIEND

BEEF — LIGHT, LEAN BEEF RECIPES
FOR CONTEMPORARY LIFESTYLES

Please send me _____ copies of "**BEEF**" at $12.95 per book plus $1.50 (total order) for postage and handling:

Enclosed is $_____.

NAME: _____

STREET: _____

CITY:_____ PROVINCE/STATE: _____

POSTAL CODE/ZIP: _____

Please make cheques or money orders payable to:
C & B Communications Ltd.
Karen Chase
R.R. #8
Calgary, Alberta
Canada   T2J 2T9

American Orders please pay in U.S. funds
Price is subject to change